Thomas Mitchell

The Old Paths

A Treatise on Sanctification

Thomas Mitchell

The Old Paths
A Treatise on Sanctification

ISBN/EAN: 9783337417505

Printed in Europe, USA, Canada, Australia, Japan

Cover: Foto ©Lupo / pixelio.de

More available books at **www.hansebooks.com**

THE OLD PATHS:

A

TREATISE ON SANCTIFICATION.

SCRIPTURE

THE ONLY AUTHORITY.

By Rev. THOMAS MITCHELL.

("Thus saith the Lord, Stand ye in the ways, and see, and ask for the Old Paths; wherein is the good way, and walk therein, and ye shall find rest for your soul.—*Jer.* vi, 16.

ALBANY:
CHARLES VAN BENTHUYSEN & SONS PRINT.
1869.

Entered according to Act of Congress, in the year one thousand eight hundred and sixty-nine,

By Rev. THOMAS MITCHELL,

In the Clerk's Office of the District Court of the Northern District of New York.

INTRODUCTION.

TRUTH has nothing to lose, but everything to gain, by impartial investigation. It was once asked, "What is truth?" but Pilate went out before the great master had an opportunity of answering; had he waited to hear this, it would have been, "Thy word (God's) is truth." This comprehends a perfect system of the history of two worlds—the present and the eternal—given in advance by the inspirer of the sacred Scriptures, and of course nothing but the consummate development, or finishing up of the present world, and the establishment of the eternal, can fully unfold the whole of its grand design. From this consideration it follows that as history fills up its written destiny, its divine authenticity not only becomes a matter of demonstration, but its outlines and details correspondingly become better understood. This revelation contemplates the present world and its inhabitants as merely temporary; the world a transitory abode, with resources adapted to sustain the transitory race, from among whom the great creator has been from the very beginning, and still is interested in it only for the purpose of selecting subjects whose nature in time becomes harmonized by adherence to the principles it proposes, with the rectitude and holiness of Divine Government. To ascertain precisely the provisions and requisitions adapted to remould human nature for this purpose, is the great lesson imposed upon the race theoretically and experimentally to learn.

That man should have been eighteen hundred years since the instructions were finished indispensable to its conception and made so poor progress, presents a sad reflection, not upon its obscurity nor upon the capacity to comprehend, but has its origin in the heart, and philosophically can be traced to no other cause than the repugnance of the human spirit to submit to its authority.

Whatever other causes were conducive to the rejection of Jesus, by the Jews, the real one had its origin in the purity of his character and precepts. Were his propositions calculated to pamper human pride and sentiment—conceding man's moral ability to cultivate and develop his own nature for the intimate society of God, in the eternal world, had he even been required to make sacrifices of everthing he possessed, even self-immolation, as the condition of entrance therein—think ye not heaven, long ere this, world have been crowded with a population? Could he even have been permitted to enter there on condition of adherence to his own opinions, formed as they must have been in harmony with his feelings, instinctive with pride, and by his own unassisted assiduity and not required to relinquish them when there was confliction with those of Jesus, think ye heaven's gates would not have been thronged, as they never had been, with saintly travelers? Or had this requirement been so modified that the opinions of other men might have been adopted as the standard of those who came after, and they not required to cut them off, though dear as right arms, or pluck them out, though dear as right eyes, when found not to have God's authorship, would not the day have arrived and the jewels, such as they were' all been gathered within the golden walls of the "Jerusalem which is above?"

The greatest obstacle with which the march of truth, or the revealed thoughts of God have had to contend, indicating his purposes with the race, has been the servile, cringing worship of the human opinion of the past, or the pride of its own.

Seeing this to have been the deplorable course of the church, which had driven it into the midnight darkness of the dark ages, the reformers adopted as the basis of their movements, and gave expression to the sublime sentiment, that the "Holy Scriptures are a sufficient guide to faith and practice." But how has this been followed? The answer is historic, and shows that not a single denomination composing the Protestant church, but which has, to a greater or less extent, outraged this cardinal declaration, by acting upon a narrow bigotry, fearing to think independently as the reformers, Luther, Calvin and Wesley did. But the opinions of these reformers are defended by such, as tenaciously as though they were divine authority.

Had Luther acted upon this principle, one thunder peal from the Vatican would have driven him ignominiously back into the deadly embrace of the "Mother of Harlots."

Had the godly and heroic Wesley acted thus, the very first onset of the enemies of spirituality in the Church of England, which at that time was dead, would have struck terror to his spirit, and left the world deprived of the great revival wrought by his instrumentality. To concede to any man, since the revelator died, and the book of God was finished, the exclusive or private right to interpret a single passage of Scripture, or to establish a single doctrine not to be questioned by any who came after, is nothing but a servile prostitution of the God-bestowed prerogative. freedom of thought and corresponding responsibility, not to man, but to man's maker. But we rejoice that we live in an age when to trammel the liberty of mind is considered intolerable, when the crafty anathemas of the bigot or the ex-communication thunders of church power fall as dead as the Pope's bull against the comet. Such a sentiment intrudes itself into the place of God, and forbids the injunction binding upon every individual, "search the Scriptures," as well as the right to criticise, not only the sentiments of uninspired men, but also those of apostles and even of angels. Says the apostle of the Gentiles, and he, next to Jesus, is our best authority: "If we, or an angel from heaven, preach any other gospel unto you than we have preached, let him be accursed." If he comes apparently direct from the courts of heaven, with a communication in conflict with Paul's original gospel, which he did not receive from man, but "by inspiration of God," and though it bears the indisputable signet of Paul or Gabriel, reject it, and let the bearer stand classified with the pestilent propagators of error.

God challenges the world to this investigation. "Come, now, and let us reason together, saith the Lord." Let us reason with a child-like simplicity, looking alone to the infinite source of wisdom revealed in the holy book of God, fearing no result to which such investigation leads, though it conflicts with the opinions of the world of mere human intellect.

In the prosecution of this task we submit the following rules of interpretation:

First. Let the Bible define and explain its own terms, figures, and symbols.

Second. Give every passage a literal construction unless its own connection and phraseology renders such a course absurd, by bringing it in collision with truths elsewhere established by positive language.

Third. The proper connection of any given passage is not necessarily that with which it stands immediately connected, but that bearing upon the same subject, found recorded anywhere in the Scripture. Select all these texts from where they stand, put them together, and you have the truth in relation to that subject, and all the light with which you can be favored, unless the author of the book condescends to give another revelation, which is unnecessary, for the present one is full and harmonious. This is what Paul calls "rightly dividing the word of truth."

Fourth. All passages belonging to any particular subject must contain one or more of the peculiar features of that subject, by which it may be identified as belonging to the same.

Fifth. The truth in relation to any doctrine must be established by those passages which speak of it in positive and unequivocal language, and those texts evidently belonging to the same subject but which only admits of inferential testimony, no inference should be drawn from them, at variance with the truths as already established by the positive texts.

Sixth. No doctrine should be predicated upon mere inference, neither upon one isolated passage of Scripture. Any true doctrine will be found interspersed throughout the whole Bible.

Seventh. In studying the Scriptures, the New Testament must be considered a commentary on the old.

Eighth. Never be afraid of results to which you may be driven by your investigations, as this will inevitably bias your mind, and disqualify you to arrive at ultimate truth.

Ninth. If you would understand the " mind of the spirit, which is the word of God," search it with the humility and sincerity of a little child; heed the direction: "Learn of me, for I am meek and lowly in heart."

Tenth. Consult no author as authority, less than divine, in so momentous an undertaking.

Eleventh. Pursue this course for life, and with as much independence as though you were the only one concerned. "Prove all things, and hold fast that which is good."— *Paul.*

CHAPTER I.

WHAT DOES CHRISTIANITY PROPOSE TO ACCOMPLISH IN THE NATURE OF MAN?

In answering this question, we propose to show: 1st. To change that nature so that it is as easy to love and submit to God's government as it was before averse it. That this change is denominated in the Bible conversion, the new birth, regeneration, a new heart, being a new creature, justification—such are called believers. They are said to be clean, pure children of adoption, sanctified; they are said to be in Christ, children of God, etc.

The position we assume, and in these pages shall attempt to vindicate is, that all these expressions are descriptive of every newly converted sinner, and that therefore they are as clean, pure, sanctified and holy as it is possible for man in a mortal state to be. They may from that moment grow in knowledge and in gracious favor with God till the end of life, and, indeed, through all eternity, but this will make them no more clean or pure.

Underlying this controversey, is the principle of God's moral ability, growing out of his relations to mankind, in view of the arrangement of grace devised in infinite wisdom and love for his salvation.

We do not mean the ability of God as displayed in the creation of worlds, involving the absolute government of unintelligent matter which had no will, and therefore no element of resistance, but in view of his scheme of salvation what it is consistent for himself to do.

The question is: Is God limited in his power to change human nature into sympathy with himself as to numbers or in degree, and if so, by what?

We answer, first, as to numbers, that he is as able to save and make holy the whole adult race, as to thus change and save a single one of its members.

In the discussion respecting the limited or partial salvation of men, making it depend upon God's foreknowledge, decrees or corresponding predetermination, has resulted in erroneous conclusions, from the fact that it has overlooked the vital question or principle upon which the whole argument rests. This requires that it was absolutely indispensable that God should have become incarnate in the person of Jesus Christ, and accomplish all he did in order to make it possible that one sinner could be converted, and that God could consistent with the infallibility of his word or law, whose voice is: "The soul that sinneth, it shall die," to bring that sinner to a condition of reconciliation with his own views, feelings and government; and thus was established the principle by which he could also bring every other sinner into the same gracious harmony with himself; that is, all sinners placed in the same circumstances, or as members of a common, fallen race.

Of course, this does not include fallen angels, and we doubt whether it included our first parents, for whose acts there were no extenuating circumstances — who had no want of balance, growing out of physical, moral or mental weakness, such as they have transmitted to all their offspring. Paul tells us that the woman was deceived, but the man was not—he offers no excuse for his sin, but audaciously answers his maker: "The woman did give me, and I did eat." That his offspring were thus infected is obvious from such expressions as these: "The parents have eaten sour grapes, and the children's teeth are set on edge." "I was born in sin and shapen in iniquity."

Every man now has his weakness, and which is his "besetting sin." Hence, as God permitted this race to come into existence with such inherited moral inability, it is easy to see that it might be made the grounds for doing for them what he could not do consistently for their original progenitors. The promise was made to the seed of the woman, not to the woman herself, or to Adam himself. Indeed, there is not an intimation in the whole Bible by which we may even infer the salvation of Adam or Eve.

We read the history of Abel offering sacrifice unto God, but not of Adam. Indeed, it seems that if it were possible for God to save the rebel Adam, it were also just as possible and consistent for him to save the rebel angels, "who kept not their first estate;" and that he has not done the latter, leaves us to infer not only that he could not, but also equally that he could not convert and save the first human sinners, Adam and Eve, who kept not their first estate. But aside from this, the great principle is established that "God can be just, and yet the justifier of him that believeth in Jesus." Thus justice is vindicated, and God is able, that is, consistent with himself, his word and government, to "impute to an unjust sinner his faith for righteousness," which makes him as sinless and holy as though he had never sinned; and do we not see that this principle embraces every sinner as much as any who has faith in Jesus? This provision of grace to our race is not only therefore as extensive as that race, but able to make every member of that race as holy as God is holy, according to the command: "Be ye holy, for I am holy;" and if it were not possible for man to be made thus holy, is it not folly, or worse, on the part of God requiring of man what is impossible; and may not every man take up and reiterate the charge of the unprofitable servant? "Thou art an austere man; thou takest up that thou laidst not down, and reapest that thou didst not sow." But instead of this being true, it is declared positively that his ability is also without limit in the direction of an entire change of nature.

"He is able to save them to the uttermost who come unto God by him, seeing he ever liveth to make intercession for them." What we understand the Scriptures to teach in regard to a man's being made "holy, as God requires," is, that he must first become a penitent sinner, feeling he is lost without Christ, and not only consenting, but also humbly and heartily praying to be saved from guilt through his name, and become conscious that his prayer is heard and answered.

This change begets in the pardoned culprit such feelings and views toward God, who up to this time had been considered his enemy, but now his dearest friend. We say the knowledge of this change is so great and powerful that it gives strength to resist all temptations, come from whatever source, to displease this God who has thus manifested to him such love and mercy. This is precisely such strength as would result if a man who had forfeited his life and estate by the flagrant violation of the laws of his country toward a third person, who mercifully and freely comes forward, redeems and restores to him both. Would such a man ever do an act to displease such a friend? Would he have the least disposition to do so? Would it be necessary for any other change to be wrought in his nature, only a knowledge of this gracious and magnanimous interference in order to secure his affection and undeviating fidelity? What temptation would be sufficiently powerful to induce him to speak any word or do any act which would injure the feelings of such a friend—especially would not this be impossible immediately on leaving the criminal court before whose bar he had been arraigned to answer for his crimes? We can easily conceive how, in the lapse of time, and especially if the intercourse between these two had been broken off by being removed at a great distance from each other, coldness might ensue, and gradually the wishes, feelings and injunctions of his friend become unheeded and forgotten; but if he had continued to reside in the vicinity of his benefactor, and also to be the continued recipient of his favors, and also that this friend had the ability and disposition to confer upon him every favor he needed, and had promised all this, would not this have the effect to increase the attachment of the latter? Now, to carry out the illustration, we will suppose that the condition upon which this friend proposed to confer any and all of these benefits was, that the man receiving them should never remove out of the vicinity of his friend, but to remain and trust him for the fulfillment of his gracious promises; and do we not see that had he complied with this condition, it would seem almost impossible for him to offend such a friend; and also that the very act of removing, or thoughts of it, from this vicinity, would, in itself, be a grievous wrong, committed against this friend—indeed, a crime nothing less than infidelity. Now, by ceasing to hold communication, the moral distance becomes equal to the territorial, and under such circumstances the wanderer finds himself acting without regard to the injunctions, wishes and feelings of him who had been, and still was, his best friend, but who had now put himself beyond the reach of further friendship or favor. So is it with the sinner, who has forfeited all claim to the favor of God, and all right to eternal life. He came to God in the name of Jesus, a true penitent, and heartily prayed for pardon, who heard and granted his request. The man was happy, and now the injunction was: "Abide in me, and ye shall bring forth much fruit, so shall ye be my disciple." The manifestation of such love and mercy captivates and charms, and gives strength to do just what God requires. Such a man exclaims: "Whom have I in heaven but thee, and there is none upon earth I desire beside thee." That this is the true idea, is shown by such passages as this: "As many as received him to them gave he power to become the sons of God," which also shows clearly that there is an important sense in which penitent sinners are in Christ's favor; and as long as he thus abides in him, there is no power on earth or hell which is either able to induce him to sin, or to pluck him out of God's hand. Hence it is said: "He that is born of God doth not commit sin, for his seed remaineth in him, and he cannot sin, because he is born of God."

While he therefore remains thus born of God, and by common consent this is his conversion or justification, he is holy and spotless from sin and its contaminating effects and consequences. But do we not perceive that the man himself may remove his cause out of the hands of Christ, which all children do when they commit the first known and deliberate transgression against God, as well as all adult Christians by doing the same, and by this estrangement they are again sinners; and as they thus recede from Christ, "the true light," they become involved in moral darkness. To such, says Jesus: "If the light in you become darkness, how great is that darkness." But as long as such abide in Christ, is it not clear that the wicked one toucheth them not, and who are therefore "as holy as God is holy," and as "perfect as their Father which is in heaven is perfect."

Peter speaks thus concerning this condition of the new birth: "Being born again, not of corruptible seed, but of incorruptible, which is the word of God, which liveth and abideth forever." Hence we see that the seed which remaineth in those who are born again, and which abideth forever, is the word of God, rendering it impossible in such a state to commit sin, in the proper sense of that term. This is still further explained by Jesus, thus: "Now ye are *clean* through the words which I have spoken unto you; abide in me, and I in you; as the branch cannot bear fruit of itself except it abide in the vine, no more can ye, except ye abide in me; I am the vine, ye are the branches; he that abideth in me, and I in him, the same bringeth forth much fruit; for without me ye can do nothing. If ye abide in me, and my words abide in you, ye shall ask what ye will, and it shall be done unto you; herein is my Father glorified that ye bear much fruit, so shall ye be my disciples. As the Father hath loved me, so have I loved you; continue ye in my love. If ye keep my commandments ye shall abide in my love, even as I have kept my Father's commandments and abide in his love. These things have I spoken unto you that my joy might remain in you, and that your joy might be full." We have in these plain teachings of Jesus and the apostles, a condition of Christian experience which is the highest, most holy and perfect, possible, and in which it is impossible to commit sin. Let us briefly analyze its elements. We remark in the first place, that it presents a standard of holiness and purity the most complete and perfect, and which therefore admits of no increase; except it be that class who are in Christ as true penitents and who have consecrated themselves to the service of God for life, and who are earnestly praying for pardon and assimilation to Christ's image and thus have commenced to bear fruit. The express instruction providing for these, is this: "Every branch in me that beareth fruit, the Father purgeth it that it may bring forth more fruit." This purging will be accomplished when God, according to their faith, receives, pardons and sanctifies them, after which they are prepared to "bring forth more fruit." Another remark is, that as this instruction embraces all who are in Christ, both penitent and pardoned sinners, and as they are thus in Christ at the commencement of their Christian career, therefore on the authority of Jesus they are then in the highest state of holiness and Christian purity which it is possible to attain, and to maintain which makes them one with Jesus as he is one with his Father. According to these instructions we learn that Christ's disciples are in him not as a mere form, but vitally, "as the branch is in the vine;" not by a mere heartless profession, or a round of ritualism, but in as close sympathy as he is with the Father—as a branch is in the the vine so that it bears fruit.

They are clean through the words which Jesus had spoken unto them. This word was the incorruptible seed. While this seed remained in them, they could not sin, or while they thus abided in Christ and his love abided in them, as his Father's love abided in him.

We are taught from these relations that if there was perfect love between Jesus and his Father, it was the same between him and his disciples. If there was perfect purity and fidelity between Jesus and his Father, the same existed between him and his disciples. If

Jesus had perfect faith in his Father, so had these disciples in him. "If ye abide in me, and ask anything in my name, I will do it."

Again, their joy was full; no joy could be more perfect than this. They glorified the Father, which they could not have done with a corrupt heart. They were not only his disciples, but Christ had loved them as the Father had loved him; here was perfect love. "If ye keep my commandments, ye shall abide in my love, even as I have kept my Father's commandments and abide in his love." The commandment of Jesus, upon which hangs all the law and the prophets, is: "Thou shalt love the Lord thy God with all thy heart, and with all thy mind, and with all thy soul, and with all thy strength, and thy neighbor as thyself." Another of these commandments is: "Abide in me. These things I command you, that ye love one another. If the world hate you, ye know that it hated me before it hated you; if ye were of the world, the world would love its own; but because ye are not of the world, but I have chosen you out of the world, therefore the world hateth you." "I have given unto them the words which thou gavest me, and they have received them, and have known surely that I came out from thee, and they have believed that thou didst send me; I pray for them; I pray not for the world, but for them which thou hast given me, for they are thine, and all mine are thine, and all thine are mine; and I am glorified in them. Holy Father, keep through thine own name those whom thou hast given me, that they may be one as we are." "I have given them thy word, and the world hath hated them because they are not of the world, even as I am not of the world; sanctify them through thy truth; as thou hast sent me into the world, even so have I also sent them into the world, and for their sakes I sanctify myself, that they also might be sanctified through the truth. Neither pray I for these alone, but for them also which shall believe on me through their word; that they all may be one, as thou Father art in me, and I in thee, that they also may be one in us; that the world may believe that thou hast sent me, and the glory which thou hast given me I have given them, that they may be one, I in them and thou in me, that they may be made perfect in one, and that the world may know that thou hast sent me, and hast loved them as thou hast loved me, and I have declared unto them thy name, and will declare it, that the love wherewith thou hast loved me may be in them, and I in them." Christ had given them *his word*, and they had kept it; they had not preferred the words of men. His word remained in them; through these words of Jesus they were clean. They had known surely that Christ came from the Father; they believed God had sent him. He prayed for them because they belonged to God, and he was glorified in them. Holy Father, keep through thine own name those whom thou hast given me, that they may be one, as we are one. No more sin, depravity, unholiness, carnal mindedness, impurity, uncleanness, or love of the world, existed between these saints and Jesus than between him and his Father. Christ prayed that they might be made perfect in one, for the reason just assigned: "That the world might know that thou hast sent me, and hast loved me, as I have loved them. I pray that thou shouldst keep them from the evil that is in the world." They were not only justified, but glorified. "The glory which thou gavest me I have given them." This made them perfectly one with Christ. "That they may be made perfect in one, that the world may know that I have loved them as thou hast loved me."

The idea here is that there is as uninterrupted love existing between Christ and his saints as that between him and his Father, and of course must be perfect. But it may be said that these saints, thus newly chosen to be Christ's disciples, were not pure; they still were partially depraved; they still had the carnal mind; were still unholy, impure and unclean, because Christ prayed that they might be sanctified, and as sanctification means to make an unholy heart holy, or an imperfect one perfect, an unclean one clean, or in other words, to do for a saint what justification leaves undone.

Well, if sanctification does mean this, then Jesus must have had an unholy, impure, imperfect, unclean, and a partially depraved heart, because he uses this term in the same connection as applicable to himself: "For their sakes I sanctify myself." Now, as Jesus had no such heart as this, therefore the word sanctification has no such meaning, but must have one which admits of such an application; and that it has, we shall shortly attempt to show.

The idea that the depravity returns to a sanctified heart by the commission of a sin—we mean the known and deliberate violation of the law of God, for nothing else is a sin; but this is a reversion of the order, the fact being that the return of this depravity, caused by taking his heart out of Christ's keeping, makes it possible for such a heart to commit sin; for it is impossible for him thus to sin while he remains in Christ, and his word (the seed) remains in him, embracing his warnings, threatenings, injunctions, promises and consequences of turning away from the living God, must first be removed from the heart. Such a heart may sin under the most aggravating circumstances, even to "count the blood of the covenant wherewith he was sanctified an unholy thing, and (thus) do despite to the spirit of grace." The elements of such a fall are, first, darkness, a gradual failure to desire the spirituality of the law of God, and to see "the exceeding sinfulness of sin;" and lastly, to lose his strength to resist temptation, and again "does the wicked one effectually touch him," and has brought him in captivity to his will. The seven other unclean spirits have returned and again dwell in the house which was sanctified, swept and garnished. He is in the condition of the branch which has ceased to bear fruit—is thenceforth good for nothing but to be "cast forth and trodden under the foot of men." "The last state of that man is worse than the first." But the most prominent feature of this uncleanness which ensues to the man, who "like the sow that was washed, but has returned again to her wallowing in the mire," is that of a perfect loss of strength; such are represented as being "twice dead, plucked up by the roots."

A sinner has no more strength to extricate himself from his moral, sinful impurity, than has a dead man power to bring himself to life. "He is dead in trespasses and in sins." And his only hope is thus announced: "For when we were without strength in due time Christ died for the ungodly." "And as many as received him, to them gave he power to become the sons of God, even to them that believed on his name." The depravity of the human heart is often so involved in mystery by the use of unscriptural and ambiguous terms and figures, that the impression as to its nature, if definite at all, is that it is something in a man as an abstraction—a being, not essentially connected with his physical, mental, or moral constitution—but the ideas the Scripture conveys in regard to it are, that Christ is the light, "The son of righteousness," whose example and precept clearly points out the right and the wrong of every question which can possibly arise among mankind. If a man walk in this light, "The blood of Jesus Christ cleanseth him from all sin," but if he recedes from it, he becomes involved in darkness: "If the light in you becomes darkness how great is that darkness." Christ is his strength: "We are kept by the power of God through faith unto salvation" (final salvation), but if he loses his faith, he puts himself beyond the reach of that power to save and that light to illuminate. Christ is his wisdom, but if he leaves Christ's school, he ceases to learn of him, "who was meek and lowly in heart," and as a natural consequence he becomes, in heart, proud and haughty — which lesson he prefers to learn of men, adopting their teachings instead of Christ's.

Christ is his sanctification; which consists in being kept from the evil that is in the world, by the power of God. Thus is "his vessel preserved in sanctification and in honor."

But if he ceases to abide in Christ, and his word ceases to abide in him, he becomes again unsanctified and unclean, which is the result of his backsliding in heart and life from God, and not at all because he did not become more pure than he was at his conversion.

His thoughts, motives and feelings become unclean, unsanctified, the result of which is his words and actions, the fruit of the corrupt tree, its natural manifestations, are unclean and corrupt.

What is more clearly and certainly taught

by these infallible doctrines of Christ himself, than that these disciples whom he had chosen were models of Christian perfection and purity, between whom and Jesus there was no more unsanctified and imperfect moral nature existing than between him and God his Father? "They are one as we are one." "As the Father hath loved me, so have I loved you; continue ye in my love."

Here we are presented with the picture of the church as Jesus formed it, and which was not confined to the disciples, but included the saints of all ages. "I pray not for these alone, but for all them also who shall believe in me through their word, that they all may be one as we are one."

It must be distinctly understood, therefore, that this was the condition of the purity of all believers when first chosen to be Christ's disciples. "I have chosen them out of the world;" "Chosen through sanctification of the spirit and belief of the truth." Such, therefore, is their purity, and such will it forever remain, unless they cease to abide in Christ.

CHAPTER II.

THE MEANING OF THE WORD SANCTIFICATION.

WE may remark that the greatest source of error, with which the world has been cursed, is to be attributed either to the wrong definition of words, or to none at all; and the error we are attempting to expose is a prominent example of the wrong definition of the word "sanctification," and if such is the fact, the erroneous doctrine predicated upon it has no respectable existence.

We have already shown from the application of the word "sanctification" to Jesus Christ, that it cannot mean to make an unholy thing or being holy, or an impure one pure. Such a definition is modern, invented by theologians who needed it to teach or prove their preconceived error of unbelieving believers, or sinful Christians. It must be remembered that before a commentary or theological dictionary existed in our world, this word was used in the inspired word of God by the Holy Ghost to teach a certain truth, and of course that truth can only be ascertained by the application of the word in those passages in which it occurs; and of course any other, or human definition which conveys any other idea than is here found, has no authority, and must be rejected. For instance, if it be contended that the word "sanctification" means to make an unclean thing or being clean, or to cleanse away moral impurity, we object, because Jesus says: "For their sakes I sanctify myself," and we leave the contestant for this definition to teach his doctrine of the defilement and impurity of the Holy Jesus, if he pleases.

The Bible definition we give of the word sanctification, is not only in perfect harmony with this application to Jesus, but also in every other passage to the things and beings to which it is applied. We say, therefore, that the word signifies to keep or preserve in a state of purity, that which has already been purified, by having been washed and cleansed by water—the blood of beasts, or the blood of Christ, or by any other process. In a modified sense, it sometimes is used simply to declare things or beings to be in a state of purity.

We remark, in the first place, that sanctification admits of no degrees, and is never used in a limited sense, designating degrees of cleanness or purity. If a thing or being has the least degree of uncleanness or defilement, it is unsanctified.

We see that the word describes something Jesus did for himself, and then prays that the Father would do that same thing for those who believed in him, who were already in him and were one with him, as he was one with the Father. They had already been made perfect—crucified to the world and the world unto them—they were not of the world, even as he was not, whom also he had glorified. They were, therefore, clean through the words which Jesus had spoken unto them, and consequently had nothing from which to be cleansed. But, nevertheless, they could still be sanctified; for whom and for which Jesus prayed, " Sanctify them through thy truth," and means to keep or preserve them in this condition. Hence also the prayer, "Keep through thine own name those whom thou has given me." Thou hast promised to "keep him in perfect peace whose mind is stayed upon thee, for he trusteth in thee." Fulfill the promise, therefore; keep those clean, and from the evil that is in the world, who believe in me and thee. "For their sakes I sanctify myself," though Jesus could not purify himself from moral defilement, yet he could keep himself pure, "unspotted and separate from sinners." He could preserve his pure being so that "No guile was found in him," so that the Eternal Father might pronounce the sublime encomium upon him — "Because thou hast loved righteousness and hated iniquity, therefore God, even thy God, hath anointed thee with the oil of gladness above thy fellows." Hence the force and propriety of the expression: "For their sakes I sanctify myself." If I become corrupt and fall, as did the first Adam, even those who now believe in me cannot be saved; if I fall down and worship Satan as the first Adam did, by obeying him rather than God, universal ruin will be the result; but for their sakes I keep myself pure—"I sanctify myself."

The word "sanctification," therefore, signifies not to make pure, but to keep and preserve those pure who either had always been so, as Jesus had, or who had already been purified by his blood. This argument settles the question as to the meaning of the word and the truth taught by it, and of course the definitions and opinions of men or angels must fall when they come in contact with the infallible words of Jesus.

We propose to examine, however, both from the Old and New Testament a number of passages, in which the word "sanctification," in some of its derivatives, is used, and we shall find this exposition legitimately deducible from the teachings of Jesus to be in perfect harmony with them all, and of course with all others in the Bible, for God is too intelligent an author to use a word to convey a certain idea in one place, and quite another in others.

The prayer of Jesus which we have already introduced clearly establishes this definition: "I pray not that thou shouldst take them out of the world (meaning not only the disciples, but all others who should believe in Jesus through their word, after, as well as before the Holy Ghost was given, and therefore through the preaching of the gospel in all ages of the world), but that thou shouldst *keep them* from the the evil." "Sanctify them through thy truth; for their sakes I sanctify myself." I keep myself from the evil. "Holy Father, keep my saints also from the evil that is in the world," and thus "sanctify them through thy truth."

Another passage relating to the sanctification of Jesus is the following, *John*, x, 36: "Say ye of him whom the Father hath sanctified and sent into the world, thou blasphemist, because I said, I am the Son of God?" Here we see that the Father sanctified the Son, but he did not cleanse him from sin or unrighteousness, and therefore the word "sanctification" does not mean this.

1 *Thess.*, iv, 22-24: "Abstain from all appearance of evil, and the very God of peace sanctify you wholly; and I pray God your whole spirit, and soul, and body, be preserved blameless unto the coming of our Lord Jesus Christ; faithful is he that calleth you, who also

will do it." These Christians are here exhorted not only to abstain from all evil, but from all which had the appearance of evil; they would thus be sanctified by the Father, the God of peace, as Jesus prayed: "Keep them from the evil that is in the world," and not from giving away to the evil that is in their hearts.

That these saints might be wholly preserved in such a state of purity, the apostle joins with Jesus, and offers this forcible prayer: "And I pray God your whole soul, body and spirit be *preserved blameless* unto the coming of our Lord Jesus Christ; faithful is he that calleth you, who also will do it. Holy Father, keep through thine own name those whom thou hast given me, from the evil that is in the world."

We see from this passage that the sanctification of these believers, for which the apostle prayed, was not that they might be made more pure, righteous or holy, but that they might be forever preserved blameless. No intimation or implication here that these saints had impure and corrupt hearts.

By thus abstaining from evil they would abide in Christ, and his word, "the incorruptible seed," would abide in them, and they would thus be sanctified through the continued belief of the truth; this would make them that they would neither be barren or unfruitful, as Peter has it, or as Jesus declares: "Ye shall bring forth much fruit, so shall ye be my disciples."

This instruction assumes that those to whom it was addressed had been converted, born again. and made righteous and holy; and their sanctification was that they might continue to abstain from all evil, and from all appearance of evil, by doing which they would be blameless unto the coming of our Lord Jesus Christ. It was not that they had evil in their hearts, and by being purified from it would make them blameless. In what perfect harmony are the teachings of Paul with those of Jesus on this subject.

There is another passage in this same epistle which illustrates and corroborates this view of the doctrine of sanctification, Chap. iv, 3, 4: "For this is the will of God, even your sanctification; that ye should abstain from fornication; that every one of you should know how to possess his vessel in sanctification and honor." And then to enforce the instruction he says, verse 7: "For God hath not called us unto uncleanness, but unto holiness." We here learn that sanctification means abstinence from uncleanness, and is synonymous with holiness and relates to the acts of Christians, whose hearts here are symbolized by vessels, which had been already made clean and holy by the blood of Jesus. Every one of you should know how to possess his vessel (preserve it) pure and honorable in the sight of God, and this preserving the heart in a state of purity is sanctification, and not that of making it pure. Here is manifested that prominent characteristic of the great system of truth; strike on one, and immediately we become surrounded by a multitude of corroborative witnesses rising up as by magic, ready to give in testimony, while the advocates of error are dissatisfied with the Bible, and in their extremity are forced to appeal to original manuscripts and introduce human renderings of words to make out their theory. How perfectly conclusive are these arguments in proof of the idea that "sanctification" does not mean to make pure, but to keep that which is already pure, in a state of purity, being the positive teachings of Christ himself and of the great apostle of the Gentiles not leaving it involved in mystery and doubt by the use of equivocal or mere inferential language, but in the plainest, simplest, and most positive terms, and from passages of Scripture which admit of no other construction.

It must be borne in mind that if we would understand any truth of the Bible, we must learn it from those passages which speak of it in the most positive language, and not to draw inferences from others, which only admit of inference, in contradiction to these. By the vialotion of this rule, everything, and therefore nothing, can be proved from the Bible. We envy not the account those who thus pervert the scriptures of truth will have to render when the great judge produces the standard by which men are to stand or fall. "I judge no man (says Jesus); the words which I have spoken unto you, they shall judge you in the last day."

Acts, xxvi, 18: "To open their eyes, and to

turn them from darkness to light, and from the power of Satan unto God, that they may receive forgiveness of sins and inheritance among them, which are sanctified by faith that is in me."

The idea clearly taught here is, that being delivered from darkness and satanic power, and having obtained forgiveness or justification, their subsequent life, by faith in Christ, was that of sanctification, their inheritance now was among those who were sanctified.

1 *Cor.*, vi, 11: "And such were some of you; but ye are washed, but ye are sanctified, but ye are justified in the name of the Lord Jesus, and by the spirit of God."

From this passage it would seem that sanctification or purity, instead of being a work done after justification, precedes it, by being washed they were sanctified, and because sanctified, they were justified.

If we consider that purity of motive and intention to serve God, through Jesus Christ, is the purity of Christianity, and as this is the state of every true penitent heart, it follows that sanctification precedes justification.

The vessels of the Temple, typical of this, God never received into his service until they had been washed clean; then were they sanctified. Whatever was in the least unclean, was unsanctified, and were thus unfit for the service of God; and it was unrighteous and criminal, by whomsoever committed, to use them in this condition. Here is the type, and we have the anti-type in the Christian Church.

God receives no sinner into his service until he has made a full surrender, and an unreserved consecration of himself; and yet we hear those who profess to be justified believers engaged in seeking sanctification, and crying:

> O! that my load of sin were gone;
> O! that I could at last submit.

Having, therefore, never submitted to God, how could they be in a state of justification? For a man not to offer his body (comprehending in this case the whole man) "a living sacrifice, holy and acceptable unto God, which is every sinner's reasonable service," is to be rejected. He who reserves any part of his purposes and affections from God, and places them on any other object more than on Jesus, "he is not worthy of him;" but if he consecrates his heart, so that he prefers the service of Christ to that of father, mother, brother, sister, lands or houses, then he loves God perfectly, and with all his heart; and God never did and never can receive a penitent sinner unless he makes this complete surrender and sacrifice, and thus performs this "reasonable service." Therefore, every one whom God receives into his service is pure in heart. Every true penitent who presents himself at the sacrificial shrine of God, with "a godly sorrow, which worketh repentance unto life," mourning his previous sinful life, having resolved to be Christ's servant for life, is already a pure and sanctified man, and for the encouragement of such, Jesus left on record one of his pronounced beatitudes: "Blessed are the pure in heart, for they shall see God," and "Blessed are they who mourn (with this godly sorrow), for they shall be comforted."

Such offerings always meet the requisitions of God's righteous law, and, as the publican who smote on his breast and said: "God, be merciful to me, a sinner," with him "go down to their house justified."

We sum up this part of our subject as follows: God receives nothing into his service but sanctified purity. Purity in his sight is nothing more or less than an honest intention of heart to serve and please God in whatever a man does. "Whatsoever ye do, do all to the glory of God." Such hearts have not only all justified believers, but also all truly penitent sinners. Such was the publican above alluded to, and being thus pure they are sanctified, and being sanctified, God receives them into his service, and this act of reception is being justified by faith, the result of which is "peace with God through our Lord Jesus Christ." It is true that the order of these conditions are brought out prominently in the passage under consideration, but it is in perfect harmony with the subject everywhere taught in the Bible. "But ye are washed (this purified them); but ye are sanctified (this is the condition of being pure); but ye are justified;" this is the result of being sanctified. That the intention of the heart is the highest standard of moral purity, is proved by the fact that it is the greatest limit to which the law or word of God reaches in its estimate or measurement of Christian character; whatever therefore meets this, must be in the most unlimited degree pure in the sight of God. "God searcheth the heart and tryeth the reins." "The word of God is quick and powerful, sharper than any two-edged sword, piercing even to the dividing asunder of the soul and spirit, joints and marrow, and is a discerner of the thoughts and intents of the heart."

It is only necessary to make this proposition, with the introduction of these texts, in order to its vindication. Men may do acts which, in themselves, are wrong, but if the motive was pure, it entirely changes the character of the acts.

1 *Cor.*, vii, 14: "For the unbelieving husband is sanctified by the wife, and the unbelieving wife is sanctified by the husband, else were your children unclean, but now are they holy."

All we have to say upon this passage is, that it uses the words "clean, holy, and sanctified," synonymously, and that the believing husband and wife here, as well as all other believers, are sanctified.

2 *Tim.*, ii, 21: "If a man purge himself from these, he shall be a vessel unto honor, sanctified, and meet for the master's use, and prepared unto every good work."

The condition here, upon which a man is pronounced sanctified, is that he first purge himself, and therefore sanctification is not the operation of purging, but describes the purified state after having been purged. Besides, we see that this purging, by which a man is brought and kept in a sanctified state, is something for himself to do, and cannot therefore be the changing of his heart or nature, which is the work of God only. Mark the expression: "If a man *purge himself* from these," etc.

This is more fully explained in the 19th verse: "Let every one that nameth the name of Christ, depart from all iniquity." Those who thus abide in Christ are kept from all iniquity, from the evil that is in the world; they are clean, and "preserve their vessels in sanctification and in honor."

Heb., x, 14: "For by one offering he hath perfected forever them that are sanctified."

We learn from this passage that sanctification is a perfect state of Christian experience and practice. As long, therefore, as Christians preserve their vessels (hearts) in sanctification, they are perfect, and if they do not again become unclean, and therefore unsanctified, they are blameless; and according to the Apostle's prayer, may remain so until the "coming of our Lord Jesus Christ."

Here we again see that "sanctification" has no reference whatever to the processes by which a man is made pure or perfect, but describes the condition of being thus perfect, neither is it applicable to any condition of purity less than perfect.

If a man has a heart divided between God and any other object, and so disqualified to serve one master, that heart cannot be sanctified, for Jesus hath only sanctified those that are perfect.

We also learn from this passage that sanctification admits of no degrees; a man is either sanctified wholly—spirit, soul and body is every whit whole—or he is unclean, and therefore not sanctified at all.

Having any remains of the carnal mind, any moral defilement or uncleanness, in motive, intention or desire, and to be such must be in heart, such a heart is not sanctified at all, for an unclean thing or being is an unsanctified one, and any degree of uncleanness is imperfection, and "God hath perfected only them that are sanctified;" therefore, to be preserved blameless, is to be sanctified, and any deliberate sin, and it must be such to be sin at all, either in thought, design, intention, motive or action, which is its fruit, is uncleanness, and he who commits it is unsanctified, for mark: "He hath (only) perfected them that are sanctified." The conclusion is, that if a man is not perfect, that is, perfectly pure, he is not sanctified; and as the least uncleanness is imperfection, and to say such are sanctified, is to use contradiction of terms, as much as to say a thing was clean when it was partly unclean, purged when it was unpurged, that a man may have a heart which is pure and impure, clean and unclean, holy and unholy at the same time. The fact is, if a thing is clean in the sight of God, it is perfectly clean; if it is pure, it is perfectly pure; if it is sanctified, it is without spot, and perfectly so. Is it not, therefore, evident that sanctification, descriptive of a state of purity, admits of no degrees? As well talk of a motive being pure and impure, an intention being righteous and wicked, a desire being holy and unholy, a thought being evil and good, a resolution being righteous and unrighteous.

Can a sentiment involving such palpable contradictions and absurdities be true? And yet this modern definition of the doctrine of sanctification comprehends all these, and so many more of equal import, that we might fill a book with them; but we go on to add strength to our argument, if that be possible, for if the truth of God can settle any question, it certainly leaves no ground for this modern idea of sanctification. We call it modern, because, as we have seen, it stands in the widest contrast with the sanctification taught in the scriptures of truth.

"Jude, the servant of Jesus Christ, and brother of James, to them that are sanctified by God the Father, and preserved in Jesus Christ."

Here again we have the terms "sanctified" and "preserved" used synonymously, meaning the same thing. God the Father hath sanctified those whom the apostle addressed, and Jesus Christ preserved them.

Eph., v, 25–26: " Even as Christ also loved the Church, and gave himself for it, that he might sanctify and cleanse it with the washing of water by the word."

Here the sanctification is put first; it is not, however, the cleansing process. This was "the washing of water by the word." Water is used to symbolize the blood of Christ. The idea is, that the church being thus washed and cleansed, Christ sanctifies or preserves it clean.

1 *Peter*, iii, 15: " But sanctify the Lord God in your hearts."

Now, if to sanctify means to make clean and holy, or to purify, it would prove that men should make the Lord God holy and clean, but as no such absurdity is taught, therefore the word has no such meaning. The idea is, let the Lord God have the first seat in your affections; let your bodies be made temples of the Holy Ghost, and do not defile such temples by setting up therein any other gods. "For what agreement hath the temple of God with idols?" Let the Lord God be the supreme object of your affections. "Thou shalt love the Lord thy God with all thy heart." "Thou shalt have no other gods before me." Thus "sanctify the Lord God in your hearts."

2 *Tim.*, ii, 13: "Because God hath from the beginning chosen you to salvation through sanctification of the spirit and belief of the truth."

Those thus chosen to salvation is explained by the following: "He that believeth shall be saved." But they were sanctified before they were thus chosen; and secondly, they believed, and it was through these conditions that they were chosen to salvation; they were true penitents, and as such their purposes and intentions were pure; and this is sanctification, their hearts had been purified by the belief of the truth; they were then pardoned, justified and saved.

That penitents are pure in heart, seems to us

to admit of no question, except by a misunderstanding of the nature of purity in the sight of God, and as required of men.

Just let the truth in regard to it be conceded, that it consists in purity or honesty of purpose, motive or intention to serve God, as manifested in the person of Jesus Christ, crying: "God, be merciful to me, a sinner;" and there never was a true penitent whose heart did not utter this prayer; this must be what it is, "a single eye," a single mind; for God cannot accept a double minded man. "He is unstable in all his ways."

We say here is the very perfection of purity. It is easy to conceive the revealed truth, that God does not immediately cast off his servants on the commission of crime, but is long suffering with them; but that he can receive one into his service who does not make an unreserved consecration of his whole being, whose motives are corrupt, endeavoring to deceive God by maintaining a divided heart between him and the world, is utterly inadmissible.

Was there ever an hour in the history of

the great apostle of the Gentiles more honest and characterized by purer motives, purposes and intentions, than that when he exclaimed: "Lord, what wilt thou have me to do?"

Was not that full consecration, expressed by Peter on his own behalf and that of his fellow apostles, and referred to the hour when they first became Christ's disciples: "What shall we have, therefore, who have left all and followed thee?"

CHAPTER III.

THE OLD TESTAMENT MEANING OF SANCTIFICATION.

Nehemiah, xii, 47: "And they sanctified holy things unto the Levites, and the priests sanctified them unto the children of Aaron."

We see by this passage that to sanctify does not mean to make things holy, but to *preserve* holy things for the use of the priests in the service of the Temple.

2 *Chr.*, xxxi, 18: "And to the genealogy of their little ones, their wives, their sons, and their daughters, through all the congregation; for in their set office they sanctified themselves in holiness."

The idea is, that the sons of Aaron preserved themselves pure and holy by adherence to the various washings required of them by the law; their sanctification did not make them holy, but was itself holiness after being washed.

Lev., xi, 44: "For I am the Lord your God, ye shall therefore sanctify yourselves and ye shall be holy, for I am holy; neither shall ye defile yourselves with any manner of creeping thing that creepeth upon the earth."

According to this passage, also, we see that sanctification does not mean to make men pure and holy from all defilement of heart, which only God can do, but it is something enjoined on themselves. Keep yourselves from all defilement, and ye shall be in a condition of sanctification and holiness.

Isa., v, 16: " But the Lord of hosts shall be exalted in judgment, and God that is holy shall be sanctified in righteousness."

We just considered a passage declaring that God should be sanctified in holiness, and here he is to be sanctified in righteous judgment, proving conclusively that sanctification does not mean to cleanse from unrighteousness, because it is the righteous God himself who is here to be sanctified in righteousness.

Chapter viii, 13, contains the same sentiment: "Sanctify the Lord of hosts himself, and let him be your fear, and let him be your dread."

The idea is, that men may sanctify the Lord of hosts himself, by "keeping the fear of the Lord always before their eyes," and even a dread of offending him, by transgressing his laws, or to hold God as the supreme object of affection.

This is parallel to the passage: "Sanctify the Lord God in your hearts." God has made the Christian's heart a temple of the Holy Ghost, and if he keeps it undefiled by refraining from the commission of willful sin, and which can only be the result of impure hearts, because "a sweet fountain cannot send forth bitter water;" and he who thus "defiles the temple of God (and does not repent), him will God destroy." But for the encouragement of such, so that they may not be driven to despair as Judas was, it is written: "If any man sin, we have an advocate with the Father, Jesus Christ the righteous."

Deut., v, 12: "Keep the Sabbath day to sanctify it, as the Lord God hath commanded thee," and "Remember the Sabbath day to keep it holy."

Here again is positive proof that to sanctify does not mean to make pure or holy. God made the Sabbath day holy, and if every man on earth should desecrate it, it would be just as holy as ever; but if men keep the Sabbath day holy, which they do by not violating its laws, then they sanctify it; hence its sanctification does not mean to make it holy. for it is eternally such, but consists in keeping it holy.

We might continue to quote similar passages almost indefinitely in defence of our position, but if any are so blinded and bigoted as to still maintain the human opinion of the meaning of this word, we doubt if they would believe " if one rose from the dead; " and we would simply remind such that their contention is not with us, but with the author of the Bible.

Indeed, there is not one text containing the word "sanctification," or any of its derivatives, which teaches the idea that it means to cleanse, purify, make holy or righteous; and therefore the doctrine of sanctification signifies not to make pure, holy or righteous, but to keep or preserve that which is already pure, holy and righteous in such a state. It teaches that every one who has become a convert to Christianity, or is born again, and is thus made pure from all the defilement of sin, is from that moment in a state of sanctification; and in fact he was such from the moment he penitently surrendered himself into the hands of God, in heart resolved to be his servant during life; and such are all kept and preserved in a state of sanctification, and would be "blameless unto the coming of our Lord Jesus Christ," unless they again committed deliberate transgression, and are thus again defiled by sin, and hence lose their sanctification.

With regard to this character, we have the following passage, and with which we close the direct investigation of sanctification:

Heb., x, 29: "Of how much sorer punishment suppose ye shall he be thought worthy who hath trodden under foot the Son of God, and hath counted the blood of the covenant, wherewith he was sanctified an unholy thing, and hath done despite unto the spirit of grace."

The punishment such apostacy merits is here contrasted by what is said in the previous verse: "He that despised Moses' law, died without mercy, under two or three witnesses."

The conclusion from this seems to be, that he who accounts the blood of Jesus, which had once purified him, an unholy thing, and thus despised the very spirit of grace, "the precious blood of Christ," the kindest and most merciful gift of God to man, we ask if such, under the law of Moses (the type), died without mercy, being the most dreadful punishment which could have been inflicted in the present life? Who can comprehend the magnitude of that which such are worthy—not only shall they die without mercy, but remain subjects of merciless ruin forever.

This dreadful punishment, which the apostle does not attempt to describe, from which fact we may infer not only that it is undescribable, but involves the idea that those are only worthy of it who fall from this highest state of purity and gracious favor with God, which is sanctification. Of course, this is on the supposition that they remain unrepentant apostates till death.

We ask if there is not here startling truth for the contemplation of those who have so far left their first love, the purity of motives and intentions which then characterized their spirit, words and actions, but who can now do things which they know the word of God forbids, and from which they would once have shrunk as from the fangs of a deadly serpent. "Remember, therefore, from whence thou art fallen, and repent, and do the first works, or I (the Alpha and Omega) will come unto thee quickly, and will remove thy candlestick out of his place, except thou repent."

We have now seen that although some passages employ the word "sanctification" simply descriptive of being pure, without that of the purifying process, or the agency used, as water or blood; yet the word is not in a single instance, of the hundreds the Bible contains, used synonymous with the purgation or cleansing principle. For instance, it is nowhere used thus: Being cleansed, purified or washed by sanctification.

It sometimes stands as a single declaration: "I, the Lord, do sanctify them," and means I, the Lord, doth keep them clean, as Jesus said in reference to himself: "I sanctify myself," I keep myself pure.

The doctrine may be summed up as follows:

God receives nothing, or no being into his service, which is in anywise unclean.

Whatever and whoever remains in his service without fault or reproof, are in a state of sanctification.

A sanctified man may become again unclean by ceasing to hold God as the supreme object of his affections, and thus ceasing to obey the injunction: "Abide in me."

The least deviation from this principle, which involves a knowing wrong, even a wish or desire to do it, whether accomplished or not, sanctification is lost, not in part, but wholly.

A sin of omission produces the same result. "He that knoweth his Master's will, and doeth it not, shall be beaten with many stripes." "Every branch in me that beareth not fruit (ceaseth to bear fruit), he taketh away." (This is apostacy.) "And every branch in me that beareth fruit, he purgeth it, that it may bring forth more fruit."

As we have already shown, the idea is clearly taught in the Bible that a heart filled with "godly sorrow, which worketh repentance unto life," is pronounced "blessed," because of its "hungering and thirsting after righteousness;" "mourning," because of the burden of its transgression, and looking for the blessing, such hearts have a right to claim: "Blessed are they that mourn, for they shall be comforted," or laboring under these pure thoughts, desires and purposes, hoping for pardon, claims that other precious promise: "Blessed are the pure in heart, for they shall see God." Such hearts are already sanctified, because pure in thought, purpose and desire, as he who exclaimed: "God, be merciful to me, a sinner;" or him who said: "Lord, what wilt thou have me to do?" who, though only in a state of penitential sorrow, from that very moment were in Christ, from which point no man could ever perish, and therefore began to bear fruit; yet God now heard the culprit's prayer, pardoned his sins, and thus "purged the branch, that it might bring forth more fruit."

That the condition of all those whom God receives as his penitent and believing children is not that of the most perfect purity, there is not an intimation in the whole Bible, not a single passage that they were ever held in any other light.

Is it for a moment to be supposed that such are still in a degree unrighteous in heart, when in the thousands of instances recorded in the Bible, where God received penitents as his children, implying their conversion, whether expressed or not, that in not one is it said, or even intimated, that they were only in part clean, and therefore partly sanctified and partly unsanctified?

As though God hath thus expressed himself: "I receive you, and command you to love me with all your heart, but you have a bad heart, it loves other gods as well as me."

I have said: "In the day thou seekest me with all thine heart, I will be found of thee." But though you now comply with the condition, yet I will only receive and purify a part of your heart; I will leave a part of it still unwashed and unholy; to cleanse the other part, you must seek me another day with all your heart, and I will be found of you a second time.

I receive you and I destroy part of your

carnal mind, but not all, and that which I leave is still at enmity against me; it is not subject to my law, neither indeed can be, neither can you take away the defilement, this is my work alone; but I don't destroy all the enmity of your hearts against me now; I will be content if a part of your carnal mind and will remains unsubjugated to mine; you may thus have your hearts divided between myself and mammon; I'll leave you so that you can serve two masters, each requiring opposite service, and notwithstanding this is the filthy condition of your heart, yet it is the heart of a justified believer. You are just in my sight, though you do not love me with all your heart, and thus you live in the open and known violation of my greatest commandment: "Thou shalt love the Lord thy God with all thy heart."

Of a doctrine thus legitimately carried out, we can only say, if it was not the result of ignorance, it is blasphemous in the extreme.

Let us here inquire at what period of Christian experience does the Bible place the highest standard of purity?

In answering this question, we will introduce

one passage, which is so full and to the point, that it settles the question.

Rev., ii: "Unto the angel of the Church of Ephesus write, I know thy works and thy patience, and how thou canst not bear them which are evil; and thou hast tried them which say they are apostles, and are not, and hast found them to be liars, and hast borne, and hast patience, and for my name's sake hast labored, and hast not fainted. Nevertheless, I have somewhat against thee, because thou hast left thy first love. Remember, therefore, from whence thou art fallen, and repent, and do the first works; or else I will come unto thee quickly, and will remove thy candlestick out of his place, except thou repent."

We are here furnished with Christ's standard of Christian love, and we see that it must be at conversion—"the first love." Of this church he knew their works, labor and patience, and with these he had no fault to find; they had not even once fainted.

And we should like to know of how many Christians of the present day this can be said, including those who suppose and profess themselves to be more holy than other men? By this reference, we do not wish to be understood as conceding the correctness of such profession, but how many, even of these, who do not grow languid and get out of patience in their labor? Do they always bear hardness as good soldiers of Jesus Christ? Does Christ know that they have not fainted in the exercise of this greatest of the Christian graces, especially if their theory of the second blessing is attacked? Do they exhibit the loving disposition of Christ toward such as questioned the truth of his doctrines?

On the other hand, do they not endeavor to crush out the influence of all who believe them in error, and sometimes even to persecution? Are they no compromisers with false teachers when standing high in authority, claiming even to be apostles? Have they tried them, and found them to have been liars, in preaching for doctrines "the commandments of men," inculcating such in preference to the truth of God? Do they not substitute the doctrines of men for those of God, as the Nicolaitans did, "which thing God hated, and which thing also these Ephesian Christians hated? Now what was the grounds of complaint Christ brought against them?

Was it that they had not advanced in purity since their conversion? Not at all.

Was it that they had not been purified from any remains of the carnal mind which God left in their hearts at their conversion? Not at all.

Was it that they had not seen and mourned over the depravity of their nature, which Christ had failed to destroy when he gave them their new birth, and made them new creatures in Christ Jesus? Not a word of it.

Was it that they had never loved God with all their heart, but with a part only? Not at all.

Was it that Jesus had left them when they were converted with a filthy spirit? Not at all.

Was it that they had not become strong and consistent Christians, who had never taken any fainting spells in any winter or summer, or who had made trouble in the church by accusing some pretenders as no apostles, or as false ones? Not at all.

Was it that they had not experienced a second blessing or conversion, which enabled them to love God more than they were capable of doing when he first received them as his children? No, not this.

Was it that they had not arrived at some standard of holiness and perfect purity of heart, higher than they enjoyed when first converted? Not at all.

No such intimation is either expressed or implied, but quite the reverse; which was that they had fallen from that high standard. "I have somewhat against thee because thou hast *left thy first love.*"

This must, therefore, have been perfect love, or Christ reared an imperfect standard, to which he bade them seek.

It must be remembered that this message was not addressed to a single individual, but to a whole church, and that church selected from among all the others of Asia, because it was in the most appropriate spiritual condition, to map out, or symbolize a whole period of the church in the gospel dispensation. And as its standard of purity has never changed, it is that, therefore, by which the universal church in all ages is to be tested.

If such is the Christian character of those who had left their first love, and who, except they repented, and did their first works over again, would have their candlestick removed out of his place, or more literally as Jesus has it: "If the light in you become darkness, how great is that darkness." Is it not clear that their danger grew out of having wandered away from that pure, unblemished and sinless standard in which their hearts were when Christ first received them?

To assume he had fixed the standard of perfect love at death, or anywhere else between conversion and that event, and that its attainment was so important and prominent as to be an equal, if not a superior experience to the first, preceded as in the first by conviction and repentance, and not to have pointed these Christians to it, as the object of their future effort, but instead to have pointed them to that love they had at the first, and from which they had fallen, is not only to charge God with folly and perversion, but to arrogantly assume to know better than Christ himself, as to what constitutes perfect love and purity. It is true, these saints were called to a second repentance and experience, but this was to retrace their wandering and sinful steps, to come back and do the first works over again, to return to their first love, from whence they had fallen, and who could not be saved only on this condition.

Their progress in purity, just as we apprehend that of all others to be, consisted in coming back to that state of heart which Jesus purified, "swept and garnished," when he first received them.

It must also be remembered that those who contend for this doctrine of a second conversion, additional to the first, make a concession which virtually gives up the whole ground.

This is that Christians when first converted, never feel anything in their heart but pure love toward God and man, and it is not until a period afterward, longer or shorter, as the case may be, that they find other things in their heart, such as love of the world, carnal mindedness, "a love for all evil," as John Wesley expresses it.

They, therefore, erroneously conclude that this was the state of their hearts which Christ had not entirely changed at conversion, instead of referring it as Christ does here to the true cause, namely, that they had "*left their first love.*"

These Ephesian Christians, although dangerously backslidden in heart, and had, therefore, ceased to be justified in the sight of God, were vastly better, because "they could not bear that which was evil," than those carnal minded Christians, who, as Mr. Wesley says, are in love with all evil, and yet are justified believers, and as such are sure of heaven. Such repugnance of teaching between Christ and man, is so suggestive that the most ignorant and bigoted cannot but perceive it.

In order to prove that the first love is not pure and perfect, it would be necessary that at the moment of the conversion of every sinner, they should feel or experience a carnal mindedness, which is a feeling of enmity against God, of insubjection to his law.

But, even if this were the fact, which all parties agree is not the case in a single instance, it would not prove the doctrine that God leaves hearts in such a state at conversion true, because it is not taught in the Bible.

So far from this being the feeling of new born souls, their expression is:

> O! that the world might taste and see
> The riches of his grace,
> The arms of love that compass me,
> Would all mankind embrace.

In the very nature of love, which is a feeling, there can be no others in opposition to it in the heart at the same time, and the individual not know it; the idea is as absurd as to say a feeling is not a feeling.

But we shall leave this feature of the subject for subsequent investigation.

CHAPTER IV.

CONVERSION PERFECT PURITY.

We are aware that it is said: "Leaving the principles of the doctrine of Christ, let us go on unto perfection." Analagous to this is the passage: " Grow in grace, and in the knowledge of our Lord and Savior Jesus Christ." These passages are in the most perfect harmony with the message of Christ's angel to the Ephesian Church. The injunction to every newly converted soul, is perpetual: " Go on, gather with Christ; bring forth fruit." " Be changed from glory into glory, even as by the spirit of the Lord; grow more and more perfect in Christian principle, in discriminating knowledge. Go on from grace to grace, from strength to strength, from weak to strong faith, but this is not to be done by leaving your first love, but by abounding in love more and more." They love Christ most who continue to hold fast whereunto they have attained, and press forward; such growth is continual, and the expansion of heart to love God is without limitation, both in time and eternity. The great commandment is of binding force on all the inhabitants of the present and the immortal world: "Thou shalt love the Lord thy God with all thy heart, and with all thy soul, and with all thy mind, and with all thy strength, and thy neighbor as thyself." This every one does when God first receives them as his children, and if they do not backslide, will continue thus to love him with the strength of all these capacities, which will continue to expand and increase in power through all the ages of eternity, and yet it is only with all the heart, from first to last, and during all the cycles of immortality, it is only perfect love, as it was when the soul was first converted and adopted into Christ's family. Here is his standard. Would to God the church might even now comply with the solemn admonition, return to thy first love; whoever of thy children have wandered from this, repent and do the first works, lest I remove thy candlestick, and thou be left involved in eternal darkness.

The increase of Christian love, and the

development of Christian character, however, must not be confounded with an increase of purity or moral perfection, because that would argue that the immortal saints would increase in purity, because they increase in knowledge and capacity to love God more and more.

In this connection we propose to show that when God does anything spiritually for a man, he is not limited by the conceptions or intelligence of the man, but does everything that he needs. Or, that when a man is converted, he is made perfectly pure in heart — perfectly clean — and is made perfect in love, because it is the demand of his nature.

2 *Cor.*, v, xvii: "Therefore, if any man be in Christ Jesus, he is a new creature. Old things are passed away; behold, all things are become new." This passage explains what is meant by being in Christ, and corresponds with what Jesus said of such: "Now, ye are clean through the word which I have spoken unto you; abide in me, and ye shall bring forth much fruit, so shall ye be my disciples." The expressions "new creature," "new creation," "created anew in Christ Jesus," implies that

there had been an old creation, in regard to which we would ask, first, if God created anything physically imperfect; and secondly, morally.

We have been surprised, and indeed ashamed, to hear men, and that, too, in public addresses and sermons, confound God's six days' work of creation with the progress of perfection, having considered it so superficially that the fact was not perceived that each day's work was most perfect in itself, and by its author pronounced "very good," which, had there been the least imperfection, would not have been true. Light, for instance, was the first day's work. On the supposition of such philosophy it would have been only twilight or gloom; but God "saw the light, that it was good."

The second day's work was the firmament or atmosphere, and was this imperfect? Was it not composed of the various gases, blended in the exact proportions to meet the demands and sustain animal and vegetable life? Was there any imperfection here displayed?

The third day's work was the earth or dry land, and was there imperfection in its construction? Was it not perfectly adapted with its grand chemical composition to meet the demands of the vast variety of earth's vegetation? This, too, God pronounced " very good."

The fourth day's work was that of the sun, moon and stars (planets of the solar system). Are we to be told that there is imperfection in the organization, suspension and revolution of these grand bodies? Had there been in the least degree, the whole system, long ere this, would have been hurled into universal ruin. A man, to advance such an idea, must suppose his auditors either fools or children.

The fifth day's work was the fowls of the air and the fishes of the sea, and were these not perfect? Have they ever grown more so? Has a single species ever lost its identity or physical organization by being merged in another? All the skeptical philosophy of the world have never been able to discover such a phenomenon.

The sixth day's work was all living creatures, with man at their head, and was there any defect manifested here? Man was made a man, " formed in the image of his Creator." Closing up this grand account of the stupendous work of creation, and it is the only philosophical one ever given to the world, God thus pronounces its workmanship: "And God saw everything that he had made, and behold, it was *very good;* and the evening and the morning were the sixth day."

For a more extended investigation of the philosophy of the Mosaic account of creation, see my large work, "The Philosophy of God and the World."

That the physical world was created perfect at first—and indeed it is nothing but a slander on the Creator to charge him with even the possibility of creating a thing imperfect—shuts us up to the conclusion, that the act of the recreation of man's moral nature is also one of the greatest perfection. Morally, as well as physically, "God made man upright," but he has sought out many inventions, by which that moral rectitude has become sadly defaced.

The question now is, did God create man originally with a carnal mind, which was enmity against himself in any degree? This is Paul's definition of the nature of the carnal mind. Was he in any way unholy? Was his moral nature not made in the image of God, which Paul explains to be "righteousness and true holiness?" But from this state of purity he fell. Now, through the great plan of God in Christ reconciling the world unto himself, he comes to sinners and creates them anew in Christ Jesus; and is it possible he leaves a part of that old rebellious nature against himself and his government—some of the same old propensities to love sin and hate holiness, a remnant of the carnal mind? Does he leave in the heart of his saints a part of the old man Adam with his deeds? No; mark the declaration: "Therefore, if any man (and of course all who are) be in Christ Jesus, *he is a new creature.*" Could this be true if he was only in part *new* and part old? He had borne the fallen, moral image of the first Adam, which was unrighteousness and sin; he now bears the image of the second Adam, "the Lord from heaven," which is righteousness and true holiness.

The change was so great and complete, through which the sinner passed when God received him, that when the apostle saw, and was about to describe it, he exclaimed in astonishment: "Behold! old things are passed away, and *all things are become new.*"

If this language does not express a complete moral transformation, we should like to know what words could.

This change does not comprehend the mental or physical nature, neither of which are materially changed by this new creation. *The all things,* therefore, must relate to the moral nature, or the feelings of the heart, which, indeed, is the heart itself, and of course, indicates a perfect change. This, therefore, is the condition of the heart, the recreative power of God accomplishes through Jesus Christ, for every sinner whom he receives. This new creation is precisely the same thing as the new birth. Let us see, therefore, in what light the Bible represents those who are "born again."

In regard to the time when the new birth takes place, and that it is at conversion, there is but one opinion. If we find that its subjects are represented as being only in part cleansed from sin and unrighteousness, and have hearts still left in an imperfect state, loving God only with a part of the heart, divided in its attachments between God and other objects, then we must admit that the advocates of the second blessing doctrine may be correct, but if the contrary be found to be the truth, then are they in error.

1 *John*, i, 4: "That which was from the beginning, which we have heard, which we have seen with our eyes, which we have looked upon, and our hands have handled, of the Word of life, for the life was manifested, and we have seen it, and bear witness unto you of that eternal life which was with the Father, and was manifested unto us; that which we have seen and heard declare we unto you, that ye also may have fellowship with us; and truly our fellowship is with the Father, and with his Son Jesus Christ, and these things write we unto you, that your joy may be full."

The condition here upon which those thus addressed were to have fellowship with the Father and the Son, and that their joy might thus be full, was that Jesus Christ had been manifested, and they were witnesses of the truth that he was the "Word of life," having seen, heard and handled him.

This is further explained in the second chapter, 24, 25: "Let that, therefore, abide in you which ye have heard from the beginning. If that which ye have heard from the beginning shall remain in you, ye shall continue in the Son and in the Father, and this is the promise which he hath promised us, even eternal life." The beginning, to which reference is here made, was the time when Jesus had said unto them, "Now ye are clean through the word which I have spoken unto you, abide in me. If ye abide in me, and my words abide in you, ye shall ask what ye will, and it shall be done unto you." We here learn that it was at the beginning, or the time when Jesus first called these disciples, and they "left all and followed him," that they were engrafted into him as the branch is in the vine. That they were then pronounced clean by Jesus himself, and while in this condition their faith was perfect, so that whatsoever they asked, they received.

To show that there was no higher state of purity, or no more perfect change of moral nature to which they might attain than that which they had from the beginning, the apostle says: "If that which ye have heard from the beginning shall remain in you, ye also shall continue in the Father and in the Son." And while they thus continue to abide in Christ, they were not only clean, but their joy was full, and had uninterrupted fellowship with the Father and the Son. If there is any greater moral assimilation to God and Christ, in earth or heaven, in time or eternity, than this, we should like to see it described; and this was the state of heart enjoyed by the disciples and those whom the apostle addressed, when they were first converted; what they were "from the beginning."

The seventh verse of this chapter shows, also, that those who had this fellowship were entirely cleansed from sin: "But if we walk in the light, as he is in the light, we have fellowship one with another, and the blood of Jesus Christ, his Son, cleanseth us from all sin."

Verses 5, 6, show more fully what this walking in the light means: "This, then, is the message which we have heard of him, and declare unto you that God is light, and in him is no darkness at all; if we say we have fellowship with him, and walk in darkness, we lie, and do not the truth."

From this we learn that those who say they have this fellowship, and walk in darkness, are not of the truth, but are liars, and are classed among those who were never in the light, or in whom the light had become darkness; and Jesus asks: "How great is that darkness?" And the destination of all liars is to have their "portion in the lake which burneth with fire and brimstone, which is the second death."

In contrast to such are those who continue to walk in the light from the time of their conversion, which introduces them into Christ Jesus, the result of which is "the blood of Jesus Christ his Son cleanseth them from all sin," whatever that means. But if they cease to have this fellowship, or to abide in Christ, or leave their first love, they become again involved in darkness, and are ranked among all liars, who, if they do not repent and do the first works over again, cannot be saved. As to whether a man walks in this light, we have the following tests, verses 8–11: "Again, a new commandment I write unto you, which thing is true in him and in you, because the darkness is passed and the true light now shineth; he that saith he is in the light, and hateth his brother, is in darkness even until now; he that loveth his brother abideth in the light, and there is none occasion of stumbling in him, but he that hateth his brother is in darkness, and walketh in darkness, and knoweth not whither he goeth, because that darkness hath blinded his eyes." The test here, as to whether a man is in the light, and therefore that the "blood of Jesus Christ cleanseth him from all sin," is the love or hatred of his brother.

We suppose the existence of this love or hate is outside of any other consideration, only is the man a Christian. If he is, and I am one, I will love him. It is the result of the new nature, and therefore, in this higher life, it is natural thus to love. If a man loves Christ, he must love every one who bears his likeness. John gives us the reason: "Because he that loveth him that begat, loveth him also that is begotten of him."

On the part of such, it requires no effort to love each other. If a lover of Jesus, when first converted, and before becoming contaminated by prejudices, bigotry and sin, which requires education from some source other than from the great teacher, whose lessons are meekness and lowliness of heart, sees the image of his master in the character and spirit of another, he loves him, no matter what else he is, has or has not. So is it on the other hand, if a man is not a Christian, and does not abide in Christ, he as naturally hates the man, and has no heartfelt fellowship with him in whom he sees the image of Jesus reflected. It is those, therefore, who are in the light, who are cleansed from all sin, of whom the apostle goes on to say: "Their sins are forgiven," "They have overcome the wicked one," "He toucheth them not," "They are strong," "They had overcome the world," "The word of God abided in them," "They had an unction from the Holy One." To them he says: "Ye know the truth, the anointing which ye have received of him abideth in you, and ye need not that any man teach you; but as the anointing teacheth you all things, and *is the truth* (mark this anointing, *is the truth*), and is no lie, and even as it hath taught you, ye shall abide in him; whosoever abideth in him sinneth not."

The whole force of this instruction, being the anointing, is comprehended in the sentence: "Ye shall abide in him." Paul expresses it thus: "As ye have received Christ Jesus the Lord, so walk ye in him." This translation, therefore, from the kingdom of darkness into that of his (God's) dear Son, is the highest and most perfect state of Christianity, which can be enjoyed in the present world. If they continued to abide in Christ, and walk in him, *as they had received him*, they would remain through life pure and holy.

We have already seen that those who have been born again are declared to be in a state of sinless perfection. "He that is born of God doth not commit sin, for his seed remaineth in him, and he cannot sin, because he is born of God." The idea is, there can be no willful sin unless the heart is unholy, because it must originate in the heart.

CHAPTER V.

THE CONDITION OF PURITY NOT INTELLIGENCE.

The assumption, that in the bestowment of blessings, God is limited by our conceptions and faith, that is the degree of faith, we believe also to be a palpable error.

Those who imbibe this error, draw such a discriminating line between the pardon of sin and the purification of the heart, that the one may be done, and not the other; a man may have his sins pardoned, and his heart still left impure and unholy, in part or wholly. According to this theory, it is indispensably necessary that a sinner should be intelligent to a degree that enables him to clearly discern between sin and its effects upon his moral nature, to draw the metaphysical line so clearly and definitely in his own mind, that his faith can take hold of one or the other at once, but not both, that each must be sought as a distinct thing; after an interval between, during which such intellectual progress must be made as would enable him to fully conceive of this distinction, so that he can accommodate himself to this nice metaphysical point in the scheme of God to save sinners. By the way, it should be remarked that this peculiar feature of God's plan is only understood by the Methodist church. It was discovered by Mr. Wesley about a hundred years ago; was never taught by Christ or the apostles, nor for sixteen hundred years of the Christian dispensation; and as no one can be made holy without an appreciable understanding of this modern discovery, therefore there are none holy only Methodists, and only those among them who are able to master this mysterious peculiarity of perception.

If there were no other arguments in opposition to this error, that it makes intelligence the condition of holiness would forever disprove it. For instance, a man feels as an undone sinner his need of Christ as his Saviour, but his intelligence or mental conceptions are not at all equal to the task of enabling him to distinguish between the nature of actual trangression and the depravity of heart which led him into its commission. He does not comprehend the metaphysics involved in the nature and degree of the carnal mind, and its relation to his criminality, he does not understand the difference between what he wants God to do *for him* and *in him*, as it is Methodistically defined, but naturally supposes that if anything is done *in him*, it is done *for him*, because his internal nature is a considerable part of himself. He simply sees and feels himself to be a sinner; that his whole life has been but one continual offence against God.

Now, according to this theory, such a man can only be pardoned; he understands enough to see and feel that it is his guilt and merited condemnation he fears, and from which he prays to be relieved. "God, be merciful to me, a sinner," is the spontaneous cry of his heart. And because he had no idea, or thought, or faith, in regard to the depravity of his nature as a separate thing from his being a sinner, therefore God could do nothing towards cleansing his nature.

We are aware that it is conceded by the advocates of this theory that God always does cleanse the nature of those he pardons, in part, at the same time. But this very concession contradicts the theory and virtually abandons it, for if God can and does cleanse the nature of a man in part when he pardons him, who had no such distinct, conviction or faith in regard to the unholiness of his nature, then he can and will, upon the same principle, cleanse such a heart entirely, without having any such discriminating faith or ideas in regard to it. We say it admits the whole ground for which we contend, or else admits a palpable contradiction in its theory. Mark, it says: God can only give what our intelligent faith comprehends when we ask, that if we ask for pardon, having only guilt in our conception and faith, and no distinct idea of depravity, God can only pardon us, and cannot cleanse away any of the depravity of our heart. Here is an ignorant sinner, utterly inadequate to any such mental discrimination, who prays only for pardon, and yet God not only pardons him, but, in part, cleanses his depraved nature; and yet to cleanse it wholly at the same time, he cannot or does not.

We can only do justice to such a contradictory theory by expressing it in the old phraseology: "God can, and he can't; he will, and he won't."

This theory questions the grand principle, that the salvation of the gospel is adapted to meet the wants and the capacities of the whole race, without regard to mental endowment or intellectual attainments.

If a man is so far removed above blank idiocy as to be able to discern between right and wrong, and that to any degree, Christ's great scheme to save him from sin, in any and all its features, and to immortalize him in his eternal kingdom, meets his necessities, and accomplishes the great work. But the theory making it necessary that a degree of mental capacity shall be possessed, enabling a man to discriminate between the degree of the carnal mind a Christian may have, and yet be one, and whether it only resides in the heart as a peaceful tenant, or reigns, and if so, to what extent; whether it is conceived of as a being (the being of sin, as Mr. Wesley calls it), and whether God could consistently chain him in the heart, making him harmless for evil, but had no power to cast him out of a place which he desired with infinite solicitude as his own residence, is simply absurd. Every man must see that the metaphysics involved in these questions cannot be comprehended by thousands of human minds, both adults and children sinners, all of whom are therefore cut off from the possibility of being saved from "the carnal mind, which is enmity against God," and especially that God's power thus to save is limited by the ignorance of the sinner. If God should reprove those who advocate this theory, it would be: "Ye have limited the Holy One of Israel."

We have now seen clearly the idea that God is limited in the bestowment of his gifts of mercy and grace to mankind, at least as it respects the cleansing of the human heart from sin, is unphilosophical, and we shall now proceed to show that it is in wide contrast to the positive teachings of Scripture.

Eph., iii, 20: "Now unto him that is able to do exceeding abundantly above all we ask or think, according to the power which worketh in us." We are here presented with a power which worketh *in us*, and of course to purify our inner nature; and now mark how, with one blow, God's great hammer of truth demolishes the notion, that he only gives the penitent sinner what is in his thoughts when he asks, or what his faith then comprehends, which idea is supposed to be taught in the passage: "According to thy faith be it unto thee;" but is an erroneous construction of the text, making it teach that God is only able to do for men, that of which they have an intelligent conception at the time they ask; that unless they have an entire change of heart, embracing original sin, as well as the depravity, guilt, and degeneracy resulting from their own life of rebellion distinctly, as separate from justification in their thoughts and faith at the same time—God will not, does not, and can not give them all these.

But mark the contrast between this sophistry and God's truth, here brought to view and its application. A poor, ignorant sinner, comes penitently to Christ, praying for pardon, lest he sink into perdition; his thoughts and prayers go no further than this: he has faith, and takes

Jesus as his Saviour. But now is he only able to save him as far as his thoughts and asking reach? No, thank God, he is able (that is, consistent with his justice he has the moral ability to do what this Scripture declares, " far more" than simply to pardon, though this is the most wonderful act God ever done) to do "exceeding abundantly above all we ask, or *think*."

If he asks less than he needs, God can give him exceeding abundantly above all that. If he asks all he thinks he needs, and does not think of the carnality of his heart, which is at enmity against God, and which led him into transgression, God can give him far more, exceeding abundantly above all he thinks. We ask if this is not corroborated by the experience of every regenerate sinner when he was pardoned. Did he not receive "joy that was unspeakable and full of glory?" Had he any conception of the magnitude of the change wrought by this power within him? Did he not sing:

> O! the rapturous height,
> Of that holy delight,
> I first found in the blood of the Lamb;
> 'Twas a heaven below,
> My Redeemer to know,
> 'Twas a heaven in Jesus' name.

Does not this passage of Scripture, and it is in harmony with every other, stand in eternal refutation to the metaphysical subtlety that God can only do for us what our intelligent faith comprehends when we ask, that infinite intelligence and goodness is limited by human ignorance, and also that it furnishes the instruction which poor sinners most need, encouraging them to come to Jesus just as they are; that if they have any faith, even as small as a grain of mustard seed, so that it enables God to reach their case, and to do anything for them, he can, upon the same principle, do everything they need, making them "new creatures in Christ Jesus," absolutely destroying all the old things of their corrupt nature, renovating it to a new and glorious life of purity and joy, of which, in all the dead past of their being, they never had the least conception.

This principle upon which God dispenses

his mercies to men, is forcibly illustrated in the following miracle:

Mat., ix, 2-7: "And behold, they brought to him a man sick of the palsy, lying on a bed: and Jesus, seeing their faith, said unto the sick of the palsy: Son, be of good cheer, thy sins be forgiven thee. And behold, certain of the scribes said within themselves, this man blasphemeth. And Jesus, knowing their thoughts, said: Wherefore think ye evil in your hearts, for whether is easier to say, thy sins be forgiven thee, or to say, arise, and walk? but that ye may know that the Son of Man hath power on earth to forgive sins. Then saith he to the sick of the palsy: Arise, take up thy bed and go unto thy house, and he arose and departed to his house."

We see by this miracle that it was wrought according to the faith of those who brought him to Jesus; and that in forgiving his sins, Jesus cured him of his palsy, although nothing had been said, or no allusion made, that there had been any thought about sins in the mind of him who had been healed, or in those of them who had brought him to Jesus;

their faith went no higher or further than the curing of the palsy, and this was done in the very act of forgiving his sins; "and Jesus seeing their faith, said unto the sick of the palsy, thy sins be forgiven thee." The pardon of sin carried with it the cure of the palsy, and the cure of the palsy comprehended the forgiveness of sins. "Whether is easier to say, thy sins be forgiven thee, or, arise and walk." Does not this clearly teach and establish the principle that if Jesus can do anything for a man who applies to him for favor, though it is only for his physical nature, he can also and will heal all the maladies of his moral being? What Christ did for this man was in honor of the faith of others, illustrating also that other Scripture: "The prayer of faith shall save the sick, and God will raise him up again."

By this example we are taught that Jesus is in nowise limited by the ignorant and crude ideas, metaphysical niceties or mathematical precision, in the bestowment of his gracious favors upon mankind, but acts on the grand and God-like principle of universal benevolence and mercy for lost men. His plan contemplates the conditions and necessities of all, under all the circumstances in which it is possible to place men. Has any lost son or daughter of the race "repentance toward God and faith toward our Lord Jesus Christ," there is no question as to the degree of either; but has he these? Can he, according to the exhortation of the prophet, in allusion to the lifting up the serpent by Moses in the wilderness, upon which the people who had been bitten by the fiery flying serpents, looked and were healed—"Look unto me and be ye saved, all ye ends of the earth,"—if so, the look of faith saves him from all the venomous poison of sin in his nature.

All the analogies of God's Bible teach this same doctrine, which shuts us up to the conclusion that if a man has any degree of repentance toward God, or any degree of faith toward our Lord Jesus Christ, God not only can but must, according to his pledged veracity. pardon his sins, and also "cleanse him from all unrighteousness." This attitude of the sinner meets the conditions proposed by God himself, and lays him, therefore, under moral obligation to accomplish for the sinner everything he needs to fit him for the enjoyment of eternal life. He is thus reconciled and received into eternal fellowship with the Father and with his Son Jesus Christ. We say it is eternal, only on the condition that the individual never removes his cause out of the keeping of God, and which requires deliberate transgression to do.

There is another feature taught by this miracle which adds strength to our position, namely, the man was perfectly healed of his palsy. A moment before he was so weak and feeble that he was unable to walk, but now he is not only strong enough to walk, but also to carry his bed; and what was true in this case was also in every other upon whom Jesus wrought his miracles; all were perfectly cured of whatsoever disease they had; and this not only illustrates, but vindicates the great principle, that whatsoever God does for a sinner, he does perfectly and wholly.

If the theory is true, that in Christ's miracles of grace in saving men, he only saves in part, then should we not find some of the cases, if not all, left on record of his miracles, one-half or two-thirds cured, left in a convalescent state? Those sick of palsy would have been, perhaps, raised off their beds, but left hobbling about on crutches for perhaps a number of years, at the end of which it would be necessary to apply again to Jesus for a second cure; but as there is no such case on record, therefore Jesus performed no such bad piece of work while on earth, and if he had, would he have earned the reputation of being "The Great Physician?"

This leaves no grounds for the inference that when Jesus receives a sinner, and endeavors to convert him into a saint, leaves his heart still soiled by sin, marred by depravity, partly spiritual but partly carnal. Such an idea casts the darkest reflection either upon the ability or goodness of God, for were it the sinner's work to make his own heart pure, he alone would be to blame were he not to do it; but as it is the work of God only, and as every penitent sinner is willing God should cleanse him from everything offensive in his sight, therefore on God alone must rest the responsibility if the work is not then done, and for undertaking to create a heart anew, and of sadly failing in the attempt.

This theory claims that Jesus had the power to bind the carnal mind of the sinner when he was born again, so that it did not reign, and that he does then destroy a part of it; but after having gone so far he prefers to live in the same heart in which this, his prisoner lives, clanking his chains, and clamoring furiously for the supremacy. Strange habitation! marvelous commingling of Christ and Belial! singular concord between Jesus and Satan!

And who does not see that this is the legitimate teaching of this terrible doctrine? The doctrine that if Jesus cleanses the sinner's heart at all, he cleanses it wholly at the same time; and that this is done when he first obtains a part in him, is further illustrated by the following circumstance, recorded in *John*. xiii, 4–10: "Jesus riseth from supper, laid aside his garments, took a towel and girded himself; after that he poureth water into a basin and began to wash the disciples' feet, and to wipe them with the towel wherewith he was girded. Then cometh he to Simon Peter, and Peter saith unto him: Lord, dost thou wash my feet? Jesus answered and said unto him: What I do, thou knowest not now, but thou shalt know hereafter. Peter saith unto him: Thou shalt never wash my feet. Jesus saith unto him: If I wash thee not, thou hast no part in me. Simon Peter saith unto him: Lord, not my feet only, but also my hands and and my head. Jesus saith unto him: He that is washed needeth not save to wash his feet, but is clean every whit."

Jesus knew that there would be some who would refuse to let him wash them from sin, and to these this instruction is addressed, namely: "If I wash thee not, thou hast no part in me." He also knew there would be others who would claim and teach the doctrine, that when Jesus first pardons and washes from sin, it is only in part, and the heart left partly unclean. Peter here represents both of these errors, for which Jesus reproved him, corrected the errors, and left the truth on record, so that there would be no excuse for entertaining them in all coming time.

When Peter found that if Jesus did not wash

his feet he would have no part in him, he was all eager to be washed, and to wash his feet was not sufficient, but wanted Jesus to wash his hands and head; but the answer of the great teacher gave him clearly to understand that if any man submits to have Jesus wash him at all, he not only has a part in him, but *is clean every whit.* "He that is washed needeth not save to wash his feet, but *is clean every whit.*" In view of such instruction, coming as it does from the highest authority, is it not marvelous that this same error of Peter's, thus exposed, should ever afterward been entertained by any intelligent man professing to be a disciple of Jesus. But it strikingly exhibits the natural tendency of the human mind to prefer the erroneous sentiments of men to the holy truths of God.

Indeed, such a prominence is given to this error, that we find it put into poetry and sung in our own church for more than a hundred years, and we apprehend this fact has been the means, in no small degree, of fastening the error upon the minds and faith of our people. Thus:

> Wash me, and make me thus thine own,
>   Wash me and mine thou art;
> Wash me, but not my feet alone,
>   My hands, my head, my heart.

For this the truth of Jesus should have been substituted, and if sung with the same spirit and enthusiasm, would have done much toward checking the march of the error:

> If I shall wash thy feet alone,
>   With the blood that doth atone,
> Every whit thou art made whole,
>   Body, spirit, mind and soul.

Can we come to the preposterous conclusion that if a poor, perishing sinner is in such a frame of mind and heart to receive any good thing from God, and asks him for "bread (the bread of life), will he give him a stone," or that which is part bread and part stone? or "if he ask for a fish will he give him a serpent," or a mongrel, part fish and part serpent? Another erroneous idea connected with this subject is that purity of heart is synynomous with power, we mean that power which enables its possessor to prevail with God and man.

Every dispensation in the history of God's

dealings with the human family, shows this element of power to have been faith, both in instrumentally subserving the cause of God and in working miracles, that this power may exist in the absence of purity, as one of the principal elements embraced in the term charity, is evident from this expression of the apostle: "Though I have all faith, so that I could remove mountains, and have not charity, I am nothing." In relation to this, the angel said to Jacob: "Thy name shall no more be called Jacob, but Israel; for as a prince hast thou power with God and with man, and hast prevailed."

The holy prophets of old, as well as the saints of all ages, have been equally pure and holy, but not equally powerful; the Christian or spiritual dispensation was to be as it has been, peculiar in this respect; hence Jesus said to Peter (referring to the strength which was to be given him), although he had been pure from the time he left all in obedience to the call of Jesus, followed him, and when converted into the gospel dispensation, "When thou art converted, strengthen thy brethren," and more definitely, "Tarry ye in Jerusalem until ye be endowed with power from on high." Hence, also the conversions which took place on the day of Pentecost, to which reference is here made, were of the most powerful character, and this was to be the example of the conversions under the whole gospel dispensation, and was there any sin left in the hearts of these justified believers? Were they not *all filled with the Holy Ghost?* Were they not all sanctified? Was there any room left in their hearts where sin could dwell? Was there any weakness, or did they lack any element of Christian experience, and remember, there were three thousand of these conversions in one day?

There certainly is no room here in which to get in Mr. Wesley's second blessing, which alone proposes to give God full possession of the heart, and fill it with the Holy Ghost, for "these were *all filled with the Holy Ghost."*

The Holy Ghost, according to prediction of the prophets, and the promise of the Father, had now been given, and according to which it was to accomplish three things:

First. He was to comfort the church in the

absence of Christ between his ascension and second coming. "And I will pray the Father, and he shall give you another comforter, that he may abide with you forever."

Second. He was to so quicken the minds of the disciples, that they would be able to remember all the teachings of Jesus during the three and a half years of his ministry, as well as to teach them the meaning of these things.

John xiv, 26: "But the comforter, which is the Holy Ghost, whom the Father will send in my name, he shall teach you all things, and bring all things to your remembrance, whatsoever I have said unto you." By this they were qualified to write the gospels.

Third. They were to be "endowed with power from on high."

Peter is a good example, illustrative of the strength and power the gospel dispensation conferred in comparison with the Jewish. See him in Pilate's judgment hall, quailing with fear before a mere servant maid, cursing and swearing that he "knew not the man." But now see him, on the day of Pentecost, manifesting a sublime moral heroism fully equal to the occasion, charging the multitude with being the crucifiers of their common Lord and master, "Whom ye have taken, and by wicked hands have crucified and slain."

To suppose these additional elements of wisdom, comfort and power, peculiar to the gospel age, made the hearts of its converts purer and holier than those of any previous dispensation, would be to suppose God took men to heaven previous to that time with unholy and impure hearts.

It is sanctified talent, full of faith and the Holy Ghost, which makes a man like a prince, "with power to prevail with God and man." A man removed only a degree above a mere idiot, may be converted and purified by the blood of Jesus, as pure as purity can be, and yet he is as weak as an infant to prevail with God and men in the great work of the reconciliation of mankind to their Maker, and any attempt at this would only provokes a smile. It is only necessary thus to merely glance at this truth, in order to show that there is very little connection between Christian purity and Christian power. There is this discrimination to be made: A man may have Christian purity, but not power, but he cannot have the power without the purity, except, perhaps to work miracles. The servant which had the five talents, gained for his Lord five more, while the one with the two only gained other two, though both were equally pure and approved.

CHAPTER VI.

THE MORAL NATURE OF INFANTS.

WE assume that the nature of children before they arrive at that degree of mental capacity to understand the nature of sin against God, is that of perfect purity, that is, under the atonement, and consequently that when adult sinners are converted, they are only on an elevation of purity equal with the little child, and that even the saints in heaven are no purer.

Luke xviii, 15, 17: "And they brought unto him also infants, that he would touch them; but when his disciples saw it they rebuked them, but Jesus called them unto him and said, suffer little children to come unto me, and forbid them not, for of such is the kingdom of God. Verily, I say unto you, whosoever shall not receive the kingdom of God as a little child, shall in no case enter therein."

Mat. xviii, 2, 3: "And Jesus called a little child unto him, and set him in the midst of them, and said, verily I say unto you, except ye be converted, and become as little children, ye shall not enter into the kingdom of God."

We are here taught by the "grace of our Lord Jesus Christ which bringeth salvation, and which has appeared to all men," that all infants or little children are made fit subjects for the kingdom of God. The fact that infants are incapable of complying with any conditions if they are unholy, they must be made holy unconditionally, or be damned.

Jesus does not say or intimate that when I shall purify their hearts, they will be subjects of the kingdom of God, but, "of such *is* the kingdom of God."

Another thing to be remarked here, is that those who are converted are declared to be fit subjects for the kingdom of God, and as such shall enter therein, and therefore must be pure.

This is not the kingdom of grace, or the principles which rule in the kingdom of God, and which enter and sway the hearts of the saints on earth, but the kingdom of glory into which they themselves are to enter.

Now, if converted sinners are still unholy in heart, a part of the carnal mind still remaining, how could Jesus say, of *such* is the kingdom of God, and if a man becomes thus converted and like a little child, he shall without any further purifying enter this kingdom, are they not then perfectly pure in heart.

Jesus here settles another great question of theological discussion, which is, that whatever contamination was transmitted to the race by the sin of Adam, he took it all away, so that all infants are sinlessly pure, or it would have been false to have said, "of such is the kingdom of God."

It follows, therefore, that all the depravity of the adult heart results from its own sin, committed in thought, word and deed, taking into consideration Christ's great atonement. We are aware that this truth is just beginning to be understood, and therefore received, but as it is clearly the truth taught by Jesus, we adopt it.

We say, therefore, that the great atonement included in its provisions of mercy and grace, all infants, unconditionally, which means all children before arriving at the age to qualify them to discern between right and wrong; hence they are all subjects of the grace of Christ's great salvation, and as all men were once infants, therefore, the whole race was once in a state of gracious salvation, and had they never committed actual transgression, would not only never have been depraved, but would have all entered into the kingdom of God.

The apostle Paul, discoursing upon this subject, shows that he understood it just as it was taught by Jesus.

Rom., v, 18: "Therefore as by the offence of one judgment came upon *all men* to condemnation; even so by the righteousness of one the free gift came upon *all men* unto justification of life." The doctrine here taught is, that by the transgression of Adam, the whole race were brought under condemnation; and also, by the righteousness of one (Christ), the free gift of justification unto life, came upon all men. As adult sinners, and all are such who are not in a state of justification of life, were once children, therefore these passages teach that the free gift (grace) of Christ justifies the whole race to life when children. That this infantile justification of life is a perfect qualification or fitness for the kingdom of God, and that conversion means the same great work of fitness for that kingdom. "Except ye be converted, and become as little children, ye can in no case enter into the kingdom of God."

When, therefore, an adult sinner is converted or justified to life, he is in that state where the atonement puts all little children: "And of such is the kingdom of heaven." Therefore, converted sinners are perfectly pure, fitted for the kingdom of God.

We are aware it is said that infants are cleansed from sin and depravity unconditionally, if they are taken out of the world before they arrive at the age of accountability. But this is disputed by the positive language of Jesus: "Except ye be converted and become *like little children*," not what they may become, or those will who die in infancy, but what little children *now are*, "as little children."

The idea that infants have impure and unholy natures, therefore contradicts this positive teaching of Scripture, and had its origin in that terrible doctrine, which declared there were "infants in hell a span long," "and that hell was paved with the skulls of infants," as it has been represented by the advocates of partial election and reprobation, which idea is obsolete; none teaches it now. Besides, if God can unconditionally purify, and make the hearts of those who die in infancy holy, without any more knowledge of the operation on their part than the infants who died were capable of having, and does not do it, then he is a respecter of persons, which he holds to be sin in man, and yet he is guilty of it himself, although the apostle declares: "God is no respecter of persons."

That God is under moral obligation to accomplish the destruction of sin and unholiness in every form in which it may exist, as far as is consistent with his plan to save men, and this is the extent of his power (moral power). Is the foundation upon which his purposes, provisions, promises, and therefore his veracity rests, and which requires him not to tolerate its existence in any form or degree for a single moment, beyond what is essentially consistent, and therefore possible for him to do in the premises. "For this purpose the Son of God was manifested, that he might destroy the works of the devil." As the devil introduced sin into the world, therefore all sin is either the direct or indirect work of the devil. That the plan and purpose of God contemplates this, and that he works up to its execution as fast as possible, is also strongly asserted by the prophet, moved by the Holy Ghost. Thus: "What more could I have done for my vineyard that I have not done in it." We cannot pursue this argument, and indeed there is no necessity for it, because the very antagonism between God and sin, and the admission of his power to accomplish the grand purpose, renders the destruction of sin, and its perpetrators, as fast as it is possible for him to do it, inevitable. God must yet reign in a purified universe.

We have seen that Christ sets up little children as the standard to which adult sinners will rise when converted; and as the nature of these were as pure as that which reigns in the kingdom of God, and as the nature of adult sinners, when converted, was as pure as that of the little children, therefore *conversion* is a condition of purity, which is as high as that which reigns in the kingdom of God in heaven.

In contradiction to this, it is said infants have inherited sinful nature from Adam, which makes them hate God and love sin. But on the authority of Jesus and Paul, as above presented, we deny this. And we care not if it is defended by all the theologians of the world, and even by the angels of heaven; and here is our authority: *Gal.*, i, 5-9: "I marvel that ye are so soon removed from him that called you into the grace of Christ unto another gospel, which is not another (it was erroneous gospel, and therefore no gospel at all); but there be some that trouble you, and would pervert the gospel of Christ; but though we, or an angel from heaven, preach any other gospel unto you than that we have preached unto you, let him be accursed. So say I again, if any man preach any other gospel unto you than that ye have received, let him be accursed." Here Paul declares the doctrines he taught to be in accordance with those of Christ, and calls on the membership of the Galatian Church to be the judge; and the doctrines he had already preached unto them to be the standard by which they were to determine the truth or falsehood of any others, coming from whatever source, or clothed with whatever authority, either by himself or any other man, or even an angel from heaven.

These Christians were enjoined not only to reject all teachings contrary to these, but to esteem those who taught them as resting under the curse of God—as perverters of the gospel of Christ. From such authority are we not clothed with the right? Nay, is not the duty enjoined on us to criticise and reject any sentiment, especially when it has nothing but uninspired man as its authority, which, in our judgment, is not in accordance with the teachings of Jesus and Paul, or which is not in harmony with the whole Bible?

We say here, once for all, that we utterly reject, and with abhorrence repudiate, the popish idea that the sentiments of any uninspired man of the past or present are to be taken for granted as authority as to the meaning of Scripture doctrines. The very moment we concede the opinions of men as authority, no more Bibles need be printed, in which respect the Romish church is not only consistent but right; for if the opinions of the commentators are to be studied and adopted as authority, and this concession, of course, rejects all but the first commentator, except they agree with him, and even then their commentaries may be treated as the Mohammedans treated the library at Alexandria, which they burned. "If what the books taught was in the Koran, there was no further use for them; and if not, then they ought to be destroyed."

This erroneous concession also forbids the idea that the Bible is the book of all ages, and which requires the development of events to fulfill its predictions, being thus progressively unfolded, how absurd that an uninspired man of the past could, and did understand its doctrines better than those who came later in the world's history. If Jesus had taught this subserviency to human opinion, would he have enjoined on his hearers the duty of searching the Scriptures?

"Search the Scriptures, for in them ye think ye have eternal life, and they are they which testify of me." It would have been, search the commentaries and expositions of the lawyers, doctors, scribes and pharisees, "for they are they which testify of me." Instead of this, Jesus charged these commentators and doctors with having made void the law of God by their traditions" (commentaries). And when the common people heard him gladly, and multitudes followed him, these bigoted defenders of the opinions of learned men, tauntingly asked, "Have any of the rulers or any of the Pharisees believed on him, but these people who know not the law are cursed?"

We fully subscribe to the great cardinal doctrine of the Protestant church, "that the sacred Scriptures are a sufficient guide to faith and practice," and to that of Paul, "that no Scripture is of any private interpretation," but belongs to the church at large, the membership as well as the ministry. Let the people become familiar with the meaning of Scripture doctrine as they may and should, and the erroneous doctrine which comes from the pulpit now would not be tolerated; in this Jesus and Paul were right, and Rome was wrong.

In relation to the idea that the hearts of little children have a natural tendency against Christ, and in favor with wickedness: We would inquire of parents, if they did not always find their little children on the sympathetic side of Jesus, when they would tell them of his heroic virtues, and submission to suffer for their sakes? We speak of little children just as Jesus has it, and who had not become contaminated by the darkening and hardening effects of actual transgression. Did their little hearts not always pulsate in harmony with that of Jesus, and burn with indignation against his foes and persecutors?

Or, where is the mother or father who has engaged the attention of a child by the narrative of Joseph, Daniel, David, Moses, the three Hebrew children, or the righteous prophets and holy martyrs, whose hearts did not kindle with sympathetic emotion with them all, and with indignation against their wicked enemies? Indeed, we venture nothing by making the declaration there never was an exception since the world began; and does not this fact present an eternal refutation of the assumption that infant hearts have an aversion to Christ and holiness, and are in love and harmony with sin and rebellion? Does it not corroborate the words of Christ to the contrary, "Of such is the kingdom of God."

That some children may very early manifest wicked hearts, is most sadly true, but, in order to account for this, we must consider the fact, that imitation is one of the first manifestations of infantile intelligence. How soon do they see the exhibition of bad tempers, impatience, resentment, deception and "returning evil for evil," and to a greater or less degree, either in their own family, at their neighbors, or at schools, or play with older children; all these examples of sin, in view of which, how can they long remain uncontaminated? Indeed, we regard it as wonderful, that so generally they remain as pure as they do, and it is here we find the great source of human depravity, and not in that in which they were born. Take away all sinners from these children, let them be surrounded from their birth, by immortal saints, and this also be their own nature, and which proposes no moral change, but exempts them from all pain and death, as well as all necessities which cannot be met, and also places them where it is superior to the Garden of Eden, wherein no devil to tempt can ever come, and we believe they would forever remain holy and righteous, notwithstanding their inherited, deranged and unequally balanced physical, moral and mental constitution, which idea is inculcated in these words: "I was born in sin, and *shapen in iniquity;*" and yet we have the positive declaration of Christ, "Of such is the kingdom of God."

This innocent, yet warped condition of the human mind and heart, as the common inheritance of the race, is as philosophical as it is scriptural.

To illustrate the transmission of this derangement, we will suppose the parents of a child are thieves, and live by the practice, the inevitable result, mentally, morally and physically upon that child when born into the world, would be the constitutional pre-requisites of a thief, his whole nature would be shapen in harmony with this vice, and the first lessons he would learn, would be those which relate to the art of stealing, secretiveness, selfishness, lying, and all forms of deception; these rapidly blunt his sense of the rights of others, weakening and depraving his moral faculties more and more, at the expense of the invigoration of those of a selfish character. The natural consequence of this would be, that the children of such parents would possess a nature more inclined to steal when born into the world, than that of their parents, and if circumstances were favorable for its indulgence, would make more notorious thieves than they. Thus, "the sins of the fathers are visited on the children to the third and fourth generation of them that hate me" (God).

Not that the children are held personally responsible for the actual sins of their parents. but the effect of the sinful lives of such, who thus continue to hate God from generation to generation, are transmitted to their children and children's children, etc. Thus, the constitution, mentally, morally and physically, is shaped in harmony with iniquity, and transmitted as an accursed inheritance to their unfortunate offspring.

"The parents have eaten sour grapes, and the children's teeth are set on edge," is a figure of inspiration, used to teach this truth, and beautifully, forcibly and philosophically explains the principle of the contamination of the race, and fully accounts for the existence of all the depravity of human nature, without running back to Adam as the infinite source of moral corruption, whence the whole race is supplied.

We will now take the little thief, and suppose his parents to have died when he was one month old, by which event he is adopted by Christian parents. Perhaps the child will not be three years of age before he will manifest a propensity to steal. The parents, observing this, bend all their energy to inculcate into his young mind the opposite sentiments of justice and respect for the rights of others. With such teaching, this propensity in the child grows more and more weak, because, according to the laws of physiology, those faculties being less and less used and excited, less and less brain matter is deposited upon them, as the organs of the mind, and the opposite sentiments of benevolence and conscientiousness become correspondingly more vigorous.

He has now arrived at an age which enables him to discern between right and wrong, and becomes a convert to Christianity, but he has not lost all his propensity to steal, and cannot, for it is interwoven in the very shape of his moral, mental and physical constitution, to destroy which would be to take his life, but is, and always will be, his " besetting sin," so that it will be easier to induce him to steal than to commit any other sin. But now he has increasing motives not to steal, and increasing strength to enable him to resist the temptation, the grace of God. He reads the instruction in the Bible applicable to his case: " Let him that stole steal no more," and he sacredly obeys it all his life; he successfully resists this propensity, and the devil who takes advantage of it to induce him into sin, and triumphs.

Now, we pronounce this man as pure and holy, as far as this strongest and worst propensity of his heart or moral nature is concerned—and this, too, is the deepest seat of his depravity—as though he had been born with an organization endowed with such a sense of justice and the rights of others, as multitudes are, which never required anything like a strong effort to prevent them from stealing, who, even without grace, would have revolted at the idea, and yet they may have inherited other propensities to other sinful practices, which were stronger or weaker, according to the nature and habits of their ancestors, and which would have always been sources of moral weakness.

Let us now inquire what would be the effect of a temptation to steal, upon such a mind, in order to prove the heart impure? We will suppose this man placed in circumstances wherein he may steal without being in the least danger of detection in the present life. The devil says steal, and this propensity of his nature says steal; he reflects and deliberates upon the act, with his mind not yet decided; he has learned to be just, and to scrupulously regard the rights of others, and he cannot afford to violate them. The good spirit whispers his appropriate text: "Let him who stole steal no more," for God always anticipates the devil. To the suggestion, no one will know it, he answers,

God will; that no one will see him, he answers, God will. In this light and deliberation he spurns the idea of stealing, and by faith in God triumphs. This is what Paul means when he says: "If thine eye be single, thy whole body shall be full of light," and is acting with an eye single to the glory of God.

The feelings which prompt the motive, and the motive itself under which he thus acts, are as pure as purity can be, as pure as any which ever actuated an angel mind.

Any act to have moral character must have time for thought, reflection and decision, which engages the will, without which there can be no sin, either against moral or civil law. Temptation to sin, thoughts about sin, of its consequences in time or eternity, are neither sin or the offspring of impurity, for Jesus had them all.

Sin implies a knowledge of the law which the act violates, and a deliberate purpose to violate that law, regardless of the consequences; "this is what defileth a man." The moral law estimates the desire or purpose to sin, the sin itself, and holds the sinner just as guilty as though he had committed it, although he had no opportunity to do so. "He that hateth his brother is a murderer;" "And he that looketh on a woman to lust after her, hath committed adultery with her already in his heart." The following passage illustrates the principle: "He that knoweth his master's will and doeth it not, shall be beaten with many stripes; but he that knoweth not, and did commit things worthy of stripes, shall be beaten with few." Purity, therefore, consists in feeling and acting in all a man does, under the light he enjoys at the time, with motives and intentions to please God, although his personal interests may, for the time being, suffer by his acts. "Whatsoever ye do, do all to the glory of God."

This is the purity of Christianity, and is what every Christian has when converted, and it is all there is of purity, holiness, perfection or sanctification. It is evident from this definition that what may be perfect purity in one degree of light, would be sin in another. What we mean by light, is a clear perception of the right or wrong of any act, practice or habit. To illustrate: it was once supposed by Christian men that they could hold slaves in accordance with the principles of the golden rule: "What ye would men should do unto you, do ye even so unto them."

Every branch of the Protestant church, and its almost entire membership, defended the rectitude of the practice, and it would be rash judgment to charge all the slaveholders, and their apologists of all past years, as being sinners. But with the views John Wesley entertained in regard to it, he could not have been a Christian and defended it, for he said: "It was the sum of all villainies." But we ask, can a man be a Christian and be a slaveholder, with the light now shining upon the practice?

It was also once supposed that every man might indulge in the social glass, and to say that the holiest and purest who thus indulged were not Christians, would be to charge that for a century or more, up to about forty years ago, when the first temperance light began to shine, there were no pure Christians, or no Christians at all, for the history of that period shows that all, not only the membership, but the ministers also, took their social glass of intoxicating drinks; but can any man do this now and be a pure Christian, or one at all? Here we see how a man may be pure and holy, actuated by the purest motives, and with "a single eye to the glory of God" to-day, but to-morrow the shedding of new light on his practices and habits, he ceases to be pure and innocent, only on the condition that he immediately abandons these and walks up to the increased light with which God has favored him. If he does this, the following Scripture describes his growth and maintenance of his purity:

"If we walk in the light as he is in the light, we have fellowship one with another, and the blood of Jesus Christ, his Son, cleanseth us from all sin."

Christ also thus describes this progressive saint: "Every branch in me that beareth fruit, the Father purgeth it that it may bring forth more fruit."

We also see that this state of Christian purity is in harmony with that of sanctification. "Preserving the vessel in sanctification and in honor," and hence of being preserved blameless body, soul and spirit.

It also enables us to understand the following passage: "Behold, now are we the sons of God, and it doth not yet appear what we shall be, but we know that when he shall appear, we shall be like him, for we shall see him as he is, and every one that hath this hope in him, purifieth himself even as he is pure." And this also: "Blessed are the pure in heart, for they shall see God."

Actuated by this great hope, he makes every sacrifice which his increased light makes manifest, is his duty, in order to carry him from one degree of light to another, showing that there are as many degrees of purity as of light, but each perfectly pure in itself; such a man progressively meets the responsibilities of every successive ray of light with which God continues to illuminate his moral pathway, from his conversion until the end of his Christian journey.

This is also what is meant by "growing in grace, and in the knowledge of our Lord and Saviour Jesus Christ.

"Learning of him," obtaining a knowledge

of the truths he taught; hence "sanctified by the belief of the truth." Mark, it is not the truth taught by men, but by Jesus Christ, taking these as authority instead of those taught by men, when they conflict with each other, yielding preconceived opinions though dear as right eyes, or loved as right hands.

We will suggest a plain test upon this point: Here is a man who holds to the doctrine of what is called "the second blessing," and in harmony with the theory, has himself experienced the feeling he supposes to be sanctification. He now hears the subject fully and fairly discussed, and weighs the arguments for and against, and finds that his sentiments cannot be defended, being opposed to those taught by Jesus and the apostles, and after mature deliberation, has the humility and moral courage to abandon them, and accept those taught in the Scriptures of truth, such a man rises to the standard of the truth "as it is in Jesus," and consequently preserves his purity, his sanctification. He thus "grows up into Christ his living head;" "He purifieth himself even as he is pure;" "The God of peace sanctifies him wholly, and thus preserves him blameless;" "He is sanctified by the belief of the truth;" "Kept clean by the words of Jesus;" his vessel is preserved in sanctification and in honor. But suppose he still adheres to his theory and error, such as it now appears, and appeals to John Wesley as his authority, does he not dishonor Jesus?

He grows up into the spirit and knowledge of Wesley, whom he now chooses as his living head, but no longer into Christ; he receives the teachings of Wesley, and rejects those of Jesus. Jesus said, "Now are ye clean through the words which I have spoken unto you, abide in me, and let my words abide in you." But he chooses rather to be clean through the words and theory of Mr. Wesley, such cleansing as they propose.

We have no hesitation in saying that the man who comes to such a crisis, and assumes such a position, and adopts such a course, sins against light and God, and as fatally rejects Jesus, as any Jew did at Pilate's judgment hall. It must be observed that we have here supposed a case, in which this doctrine has been examined according to the light which now, or at any time shines upon it. He has seen, for instance, that the words of Jesus do not teach that a man must seek sanctification or purity, after being converted, just as he sought justification, but that it is the result of his conversion or justification; that the Bible does not enjoin it as a duty to make a distinct profession of sanctification, not to do which is to lose it. He sees that no apostle or disciple ever left on record such a profession. That the great apostle of the Gentiles said of himself, "I am the chief of sinners." That none ever said, I am sanctified, I am perfect, I am pure, I am clean, I am holy, I am better than other men. It is true, he may find one profession in the sacred record bearing a striking resemblance to it. *Luke*, xviii: "One of the scribes stood and prayed thus with himself: 'God, I thank thee that I am not as other men.'"

This called out the following criticism of Jesus: "And he spake this parable unto certain which trusted in themselves that they were righteous and despised others." Instead of of thus parading their own righteousness.

We have also the following instruction from Paul, *Phil.*, 2, 3, 5: "Let nothing be done through vain glory, but in lowliness of mind let each esteem other better than themselves; let this mind be in you which was also in Christ Jesus."

But we would ask if those professing the second blessing, do not reverse all this, and instead of esteeming others better than themselves, absolutely esteem the altar or anxious seat the only appropriate place for all others but themselves?

Now, we ask again, after mature and impartial investigation, which is the test to which every man should submit his sentiments? We are convinced this doctrine, so repugnant to the spirit and letter of Christianity, can still be maintained, and the individual preserve his purity and reverence for the words of Jesus. Can he prefer the teachings of men to those of Christ and the apostles, and be innocent?

CHAPTER VII.

MR. WESLEY'S SERMONS, "SIN IN BELIEVERS," REVIEWED.

We now propose to consider the arguments in favor of this doctrine, contained in two of Mr. John Wesley's sermons, entitled "Sin in Believers, and Repentance of Believers." To suppose Mr. Wesley's teachings free from error, is to suppose him not human. And it is difficult for us to conceive how a mind so logical, possessing an intelligence so broad and diversified, could have been the author of this theory, and with no better proof could have been satisfied with its correctness.

The circumstance which gave rise to the preparation and preaching of these sermons was, that a man by the name of Zinzendorf had been preaching that when God converted a sinner he made a perfect work of it, cleansing his heart from all sin and unrighteousness, as well as pardoning his transgressions.

Mr. Wesley gives the following description of the hearts of believers who are in a state of justification at and after conversion. We quote from the sermons without giving the page. He says: "It is true that when they (sinners) first pass from death unto life, they desire nothing more but God. 'Whom have I in heaven but thee, and there is none upon earth I desire beside thee;' but it is not always so.

"Every one feels the love of the world sooner or later. Every believer, even from the moment of his justification, has in his heart pride, self-will, contrary to the will of God, covetousness, envy, the carnal mind, love of the world, and all evil—are lovers of pleasure more than lovers of God.

"A conviction of this sin remaining in their hearts is the repentance of believers.

"A conviction of their guiltiness is another branch of that repentance which belongs to the children of God.

"A man may be in the favor of God, though he feels sin, but not if he yields to it, feeling sin does not forfeit the favor of God, giving way to it does."

This attempt at the reconciliation of such incongruous ideas, we can consider in no other light than mere sophistry, having no real foundation either in reason or Scripture. It will be seen that Mr. Wesley's whole argument rests on the proposition that the sins known by these names may exist in the heart and not be yielded to.

In opposition to this we assume, and shall attempt to prove, this to be unphilosophical and unscriptural.

Our first argument is, that these terms express active principles, and it would be as reasonable to suppose the inactive existence of fire as that these can be in the heart and not actuate the man. It is their activity which gives them existence, and what gives them activity is, that the heart furnishes material for consumption.

In order to illustrate this principle, it is necessary to examine the terms thus used as they stand recorded in the Bible; and as they are the words which the "Holy Ghost useth," we appeal to him for a definition of their meaning.

We take first that of unbelief. Belief and unbelief express exercise of the mind and heart, as well as opposite principles.

The indispensable condition of belief or unbelief is knowledge. A man, therefore, can have no belief or unbelief in regard to a matter concerning which he is entirely ignorant. The mere statement of this proposition is sufficient for its vindication. A mind can only believe upon evidence, and of course can only disbelieve after the investigation of the evidence within his reach; and this disbelief is the rejection of the evidence, and a refusal to act in accordance with it is infidelity; first, to the man's own convictions; and secondly, to him who requires different action. And what makes it unbelief is the result of this mental exercise and determination.

If the subject upon which the exercise is had is the claims of God upon the individual, the rejection of the evidence is unbelief, and this unbelief is sin, from which it follows that there can be no unbelief in the heart as a harmless or innocent thing.

In confirmation of this view, we find every passage of Scripture containining the words doubt or unbelief to signify sin, and consequent condemnation, and that, too, without regard to the individual, whether professing to be a Christian or not. The only discrimination is against those who profess to be the children of God. Unbelief in the hearts of these is intensely more wicked in the estimation of God, because they thus sin against the greater light. We introduce a few of these passages to illustrate:

Rom. xiv, 23: "And he that doubteth is damned (condemned) if he eat, because he eateth not with faith, for whatsoever is not of faith is sin." There is no room here to get in Mr. Wesley's guiltless unbelief. It is not how much he doubts, but if he doubt at all he is a condemned sinner.

Heb. iii, 12: "Take heed, brethren, lest there be in any of you an evil heart of unbelief, in departing from the living God." Here Paul's brethren were in danger of having their hearts becoming unbelieving, and if they did, it would not be a quiescent, but an active, moving, *evil heart,* " departing from the living God," where unbelief exists. Such is its work; and if it exists in the heart of a man at the moment of his conversion, then he begins at that moment to "depart from the living God." It is the very nature of such an evil heart to go away from God."

Chapter iv, 11: "Let us labor, therefore, to enter into that rest, lest any man fall after the same example of unbelief," To have unbelief, therefore, is to fall from the favor of God, and forfeits the right to enter into eternal rest. But it is needless to continue these quotations, for there is not in the whole Bible the description of a heart which had unbelief, but was also a sinful heart. There are a few apparent exceptions, but we shall see they are not real.

Pride is another of these sins. This also must be active to exist. To talk about pride in the heart chained, and therefore harmless, is to suppose it to be a person, abstract from the heart itself, which is only its tenement, and not a principle.

Pride and humility are opposite and express feelings of the heart, which feelings are part of the heart itself; and is it not nonsense to talk about inactive feelings? Indeed, pride comes into existence by the yielding of the heart in a forbidden direction, and therefore without this yielding it cannot exist; and the heart in which it exists can only be a sinful one. It is the sin which universally rejects God.

Of those having such hearts it is said: "The proud the Lord knoweth afar off; and all the proud, and all that do wickedly, shall be stubble, and the day that cometh shall burn them up, saith the Lord of Hosts, that it shall leave them neither root nor branch." Just in the degree in which pride exists in the heart, that heart, says God, shall not reign over it; and if it was there when that heart was converted, God accepted it with such a reservation, the mere supposition of which is shocking.

"Covetousness" is another of the sins Mr. Wesley says is in the hearts of all mere justified believers. Covetousness is not the desire to possess the necessities and even the comforts of life. For this opinion we have the highest authority.

Mark x, 29–30: "And Jesus answered and said: Verily, I say unto you, there is no man that hath left house, or brethren, or sister, or father, or mother, or wife, or children, or lands, for my sake and the gospel's, but he shall receive a hundred-fold now in this time, houses, and brethren, and sisters, and mothers, and children, and lands, with persecutions, and in the world to come eternal life."

The holiest saint may therefore earnestly desire all these, and when he prays for them, his faith rests on the veracity of Jesus for their bestowment. There is a sense in which covetousness, although an active principle of the mind and heart, may be indulged, and the individual not only remain innocent but commendable. Hence Paul says: "Covet, therefore, earnestly the best gifts." This honors God by acknowledging the infinitude of his resources, and willingness to supply all the wants of his saints; but if a man earnestly desires and prays for the possessions of his neighbor, it shows he does not love his neighbor as himself, for "love worketh no ill to its neighbor;" and this disposition would selfishly impoverish him. He who does this, sins against God and his neighbor both, and violates the last commandment in the Decalogue: *Ex.* xx, 17: "Thou shalt not covet thy neighbor's house, nor his wife, nor his man-servant, nor his maid-servant, nor his ox, nor his ass, nor anything that is thy neighbor's."

Paul designates it idolatry—"covetousness, which is idolatry." Sinful covetousness, therefore, is a desire to possess anything belonging to a man's neighbor without paying an equivalent for it, no matter how small the value of the thing, but does not go so far as to possess it; to do this would be the violation of another commandment: "Thou shalt not steal." We see from this that covetousness, which is a desire of the heart, cannot exist unless the heart yields to it; the desire is the covetousness, and this is sin, and to talk about an inactive desire is absurd, and therefore false.

Mr. Wesley also says a believer, if he is only justified, has the love of the world in his heart; but Jesus says: "If any man love the world, the love of the Father is not in him."

He also says justified believers are "lovers of pleasure more than lovers of God;" but Paul says, that "lovers of pleasure only have the form of godliness, but deny the power thereof," and warns Christians to "turn away from such." Such, therefore, are not justified believers. From this review, is it not perfectly evident that those who have these sins in their hearts, are not justified believers, but sinners against God? They may have been backsliders "who departed from the living God;" or they may have never known the way. In either case it is the same, and there is not a passage of Scripture which can be produced, which declares any man having any of these sins in his heart in any degree, is in a justified state, or that he is a justified believer, or that he is a believer at all.

It must be distinguished between a temptation to covetousness and covetousness itself. If so tempted, the man has time to deliberate after the suggestion is made to his mind; time for instance, to reflect thus: If I were in my neighbor's place, would I be willing he should take my property without compensation; if not, how can I thus desire his without the infringement of the golden rule; besides God says "thou shalt not covet," and to do it, would be to incur his displeasure. His heart now revolts at the thought, and has no desire for that which belongs to another, or to obtain it in any dishonest manner; he "resists the devil and he flees from him," and in the contest remains pure and uncontaminated. Jesus himself was in all points tempted as we are, and he also reasoned with the tempter, and yet without sin.

That under the temptation, a man has time to deliberate before he becomes in the least infected by sin, the following passage fully proves: *James* i, 14, 15: "But every man is tempted, when he is drawn away of his own lust, and enticed, then when lust hath conceived, it bringeth forth sin; and sin when it is finished, bringeth forth death." This is no peculiar temptation, but the general principle, that of every man's temptation, to whom it is presented, conducted and consummated. A man is enticed by a suggestion from satan, or from any other source, to dishonestly possess himself of something belonging to another; thus far, it is not his sin, but that of the tempter. He now reflects upon the principle of unrighteousness involved in it, and considers the consequences, but if he has no desire to perpetrate the act, and a desire can only result from reflection, and repels the suggestion, he is still innocent. But, if after thus reflecting, he feels a desire or lust to thus wrong his neighbor, it is the conception of sin (the sin of covetousness), and when the sin is finished, death is the consequence, but the heart of such a man, if he thus resists, remains as pure and holy as it is possible for man to be in the present life, being in that condition only in which he is susceptible, because human, of yielding to temptation. Another condition of the heart of a believer, according to Mr. Wesley, "is that of carnal mindedness, and a love of all evil."

We confess, that even to write these words seems horrible, for even the devil himself can have no worse heart than to be in *love with all evil*, and especially that such is the heart of every justified believer.

We cannot but suspect the heart of any man who honestly and intelligently makes such assertions. A man can only say this from observation and experience, and as it relates to the condition of the hearts of others, which may never go so far as to be manifested in acts; therefore, no man can thus judge of others. Of course, he must know whether it was the condition of his own heart when he was first justified, or when he supposed he was, but unless we disregard all the teachings of Jesus and the apostles, relative to the state of the heart when God first received it, we cannot but conclude, either that Mr. Wesley was never justified, or that such was not the state of his heart at that event, the latter opinion being the only one upon which we are able to account for his representations of the hearts of all justified believers, and especially his own, and indeed, this was the only heart of which he was capable of judging correctly, for none but God knows what is in the heart, unless it manifests itself in the fruits, and we cannot believe that such was the condition of his heart when God converted it, and if all, or any of these sins were found in it at any time after his conversion, it is positive proof that he had become backslidden in heart. "As he had received Christ Jesus the Lord, he had ceased to walk in him."

This text, by the way, overthrows his whole theory, for it sets up the condition of the heart when it first received Christ Jesus, the Lord, which was conversion, as the standard to be maintained through life. "As ye have received him, *so walk ye in him.*" If when ye received Christ into your hearts, ye were not sanctified, but were left impure and unholy in heart, then *so walk ye in him,* so remain through all life's journey, with unclean and unsanctified hearts. But if Paul did not teach such revolting sentiments as these, he must have taught the opposite ones, namely, "As ye have received Christ Jesus, the Lord, so walk ye in him," which language could only have been applicable to sanctified human nature, "*so walk ye in him,*" look for no higher standard of purity; if you ever stray from this, "*repent and do the first works over again.*" You may forever grow in grace, but not out of sin; this is the work of God's translating power, but when in grace, then grow on in it, and in the knowledge of Christ forever. Eternity will never enable a man to comprehend the great character of Christ, but this is not growing in purity; when

God changes the heart, "old things pass away, and all things become new."

It is possible that Mr. Wesley's theory of the being of sin deceived himself, supposing as he did, it to be a personal abstraction, a being who might be in the heart as food is in the stomach, susceptible of being enthroned or dethroned, bound with chains, or loosed.

In support of the assumption that all mere justified believers have carnal minds, Mr. Wesley quotes a part of the following Scripture: 1 *Cor.* iii, 1–3: "And I, brethren, could not speak unto you as unto spiritual, but as unto carnal, even as unto babes in Christ. I have fed you with milk, and not with meat, for hitherto ye were not able to bear it; neither yet now are ye able; for are ye not carnal? For whereas there is among you envying and strife, and divisions, are ye not carnal, and walk as men? For while one saith, I am of Paul, and another, I am of Apollos, are ye not carnal?" In regard to this carnal-mindedness, we remark that it was not an innocent condition of the heart, as assumed by Mr. Wesley, and that it existed, but did not reign—was there simply as a dethroned king, bound in chains, but was there according to the philosophy of Jesus, thus: "Out of the abundance of the heart the mouth speaketh."

There was envying, divisions and strife among them, thus were they carnal. The carnality did not silently exist in their hearts, but showed itself openly among them, which called out the rebuke of the apostle: "Are ye not carnal and walk as men (other men, sinners)?"

Mr. Wesley says: "There does still remain, even in them that are justified, a mind which is in some measure carnal, so the apostle tells even the believers at Corinth;" and then goes on to call it a propensity to pride, self-will, anger, revenge, love of the world, and all evil. But he only quotes from this letter as far as was convenient to make out a theory.

Paul does not charge these Corinthians with having a propensity of heart to envy, strife and divisions, but that they were carnal, because they committed these sins.

James defines them thus, iii, 14–16: "But if ye have bitter envying and strife in your hearts, glory not, and lie not against the truth;

this wisdom descendeth not from above, but is earthly, sensual, devilish; for where envying and strife is, there is confusion and every evil work."

It is very plain to see from this that the carnal mind in these professors was not an evil propensity, but meant those evil works which originated from beneath, and were sensual, earthly and devilish, and not simply "propensities."

Another remark we wish here to make is, that the whole church of Corinth were not thus carnal; some were, while others were spiritual; some were perfect, some were sanctified, to whom reference is thus made: Chapter ii, 6: "Howbeit we speak wisdom among them that are perfect?" Chapter i, 30: "But of him *are ye in Christ Jesus*, who of God is made unto us wisdom, righteousness, sanctification and redemption." Chapter i, 7–8: "Even as the testimony of Christ was confirmed in you, so that ye came behind in no gift, waiting for the coming of our Lord Jesus Christ, who shall also confirm you unto the end, that ye may be blameless in the day of our Lord Jesus Christ."

From these various passages of the same letter, can anything be more evident than that there were two classes in the church at Corinth, as there always were, and are, in every church. even when composed of the twelve apostles it had in it, a profane and lying Peter, and a carnal minded Judas.

If Mr. Wesley had conceived and acknowledged this fact, in regard to the Corinthian church, he would have found no evidence in this letter for his theory of carnal hearted and yet justified believers.

It is also conclusive from the meaning of the words " carnal minded," that in no degree can it exist in the heart of a justified child of God. That if it exists, it must be active; this action is sin against God, and classifies its subjects as God's enemies.

In regard to the meaning of the words of Scripture, we uttterly repudiate the idea of appealing to dictionary makers, human renderings, original mapuscripts or other translations, than our own Bible as we have it now in English. There is not an idea God ever revealed to man nesessary for his perfect understanding of the purposes of the Deity with the race but what it contains.

We hold that it has been as absolutely necessary for the interference of the author of the Bible, when it was to undergo translation in order to preserve it pure and uncorrupted, as to first inspire the prophets to write it. This is especially true of the words themselves.

Words are signs of ideas, and the words of Scripture are the signs of God's ideas, which express his will concerning man. If, therefore, men may change *these words*, so as to make them convey other ideas, in any degree different, signifying less or more, then in the same degree God's ideas are changed, and the Bible ceases to be an inspired revelation of the will of God to man.

In a word, he has abandoned his word, after having been engaged more than four thousand years in inspiring men to write it, to the mere cupidity, bigotry and ignorance of men. A mere human author, having a copyright to a book, would never suffer another to change and corrupt it, and then palm it on the world as the original, without protest and rebuke; and is it not monstrous to suppose God can thus submit his great book, containing the rule of the last great judgment, to be so corrupted and changed that it could not be used for the purpose? No; the very thought is terrible to contemplate.

Jesus says: "Not a jot or tittle shall in anywise pass from the law till all be fulfilled." And can a jot or tittle any more pass from the prophesies which "came not by the will of men, but were written by holy men of God, as they were moved by the Holy Ghost?"

Paul puts it thus: 1 *Cor.* ii, 12–13: "Now we have received not the spirit of the world, but the spirit which is of God, that we might know the things which are freely given to us of God, which things also we speak, not in the *words* which man's wisdom teacheth, but which the Holy Ghost teacheth, comparing spiritual things with spiritual."

It is true there are what purports to be versions of the Scriptures, whose words are not exactly alike, and which convey different meanings. Such is what is called the Douay Bible, or that sanctioned by the Roman Catholic

Church. But in our opinion it is too corrupt, ever to come into general use. It is appropriate enough for that corrupt church, who has very little use for a Bible, if any, indeed, which would prefer that there were none, at least since the "holy fathers" died, whose doctrines constitute the infallible sentiments of the Romish church, which has "chosen to believe a lie, and to have pleasure in unrighteousness."

When it became necessary by the progress of the Reformation to have the Bible correctly translated, God, its author, had the great council under the order of King James, assembled, through whose instrumentality he blessed the world with the uncorrupted Bible.

To illustrate our idea: suppose the Mormons should translate the Bible, and make it teach their doctrines. They might succeed, but the production would be confined to that corrupt body.

Suppose the Baptists should translate the Bible, and substitute the word immersion for that of baptism, the book would forever be confined to that sect, and only the most bigoted, and therefore, the most ignorant among them, would have any more reverence for it than for any other human production.

Suppose the Methodist church should translate the Bible, and make the word sanctification mean to purify and cleanse from sin a portion, but a very small one, would receive it, but it could never come into general use, even among ourselves.

A natural inference from this is, that when it is necessary to appeal to other versions and original manuscripts to establish any theory, or prove any doctrine, that doctrine or theory is an error; and in every case when a man is heard to appeal to these in support of any opinion, that opinion or idea has a phase of meaning not only not taught in the Bible, but contrary to it.

Indeed, such a course supposes every man to have the right to translate the Bible, or to make one to suit himself, and which also implies our Bible corrupt, and that any man can make a purer one, and therefore, that God has no Bible at all, but a corrupt one, and of course, of which he cannot be the author. What can be greater presumption?

We return again to the question, as to what we are to understand by the words "to be carnally minded?" *Rom.* viii, 6, 7: "For to be carnally minded is death; but to be spiritually minded is life and peace; because the carnal mind is enmity against God; for it is not subject to the law of God, neither indeed can be."

This was the condition of those whom Paul personates in the seventh chapter, 14, 15: "For we know the law is spiritual, but I am carnal, sold under sin, for that which I do I allow not; for what I would, that I do not, but what I hate that do I."

This definition of carnality forbids the idea that it is something which may exist in the heart, in a passive and inoperative condition, because it is itself, an active principle or feeling, and that feeling "is enmity against God." It follows, therefore, that if there is no enmity felt against God in the heart, there is no carnal mind there, because the carnal mind is a feeling, and that feeling "*is enmity against God*," and can anything be more absurd than the supposition that enmity against God, one of the strongest passions of the human spirit, and which is only another phrase to express the carnal mind itself, can exist in the heart, as Mr. Wesley says it does at conversion, and the individual not know it, and also that it can thus exist, and not reign and govern its possessor?

There may be degrees of its intensity, some may have minds more bitterly at enmity against God than others, but in the precise degree in which it exists, it is a feeling, and feeling is emotion, *activity*, and that feeling is "enmity against God." Such, therefore, is the definition of the carnal mind, if Paul is to be taken as authority in preference to Mr. Wesley, or any other man. It is due to him to say that he avoids its definition thus given. If there is a sentence composed of the same number of words, capable of describing as bad and wicked a mind as this, we care not whether it is that of man or devil, we are utterly unable from the vocabulary to select them. "*The carnal mind is enmity against God.*"

Let it be understood, therefore, that if the views of Mr. Wesley are correct, every new born soul has in his heart, and that is the most hateful place in the sight of God to have it, "*enmity against God.*"

Not that he may commit some abominable act, ignorantly or in a passion, under severe provocation, but the enmity is abiding in his heart, and not only so, but its malignity is not turned simply against his brother, which God holds to be equal to murder, "For he that hateth his brother is a murderer." But the enmity is against God himself, the God of love and mercy, who has just manifested himself as such, in graciously pardoning and absolving the guilty wretch from all his sins, and in return receives the enmity of his heart against himself. God said to him, "Son give me thy heart," but he has reserved a part of it, in which enmity against God may live. O! God, how can man charge thee with being the author of such horrid doctrine? But Paul also says: "The carnal mind is not subject to the law of God." Therefore, every young convert, according to Mr. Wesley, has a mind which is only in part subject to the law of God, and of course, the other part is in rebellion against him.

The proposition God makes to a sinner is: "In the day thou seekest me with all thy heart, I will be found of thee." But here are sinners who have sought him with only a part of the heart, or if they sought him with all the heart, he only received a part. In either case the sinner maintains to some extent, the carnal mind, and to that extent has a mind "not subject to the law of God."

Is it not evident from this, that if God is found of such hearts, he must materially modify this condition of reception, which would then read: In the day thou seekest me with part of thy heart, I will be found of thee, and if you seek me with all your heart, I will accept in that day only a part; I propose to leave a part of it still in a state of enmity against myself, and of insubordination to my reign and laws. But this is not all of the apostle's description of this dreadful state of mind, for he also says: The carnal mind is not only not subject to the law of God, but declares it cannot be, "neither indeed can be."

God can convert a covetous heart, and sanctify it, by setting it apart for himself, so that it will cease to covet its neighbor's property, and covet that only which belongs to God, and which he has promised to bestow; thus, "covet earnestly, therefore, the best gifts."

He can take a jealous heart and convert it without destroying it, by turning that feeling into holy exercise, "A godly jealousy." But the carnal mind is of such a satanic composition, that there is no purpose to which infinite wisdom can appropriate it; its nature is so hateful, audacious and ungovernable that God cannot make it subservient to his will and law. "The carnal mind is not subject to the law of God, neither, indeed *can be*." And yet, according to Mr. Wesley, this terrible principle in some degree is in the heart of every child of God, even from the moment of conversion, which is the condition of the hearts of all merely justified believers, and he qualifies this by declaring them to be "in love with all evil." In proof of this, he appeals to the following passage: "The flesh lusteth against the spirit, and the spirit against the flesh," in the various forms in which it occurs in the writings of Paul, maintaining that it expresses the condition of all mere justified believers, but we think it has no reference to Christian experience.

CHAPTER VIII.

CONTINUATION OF THE SAME SUBJECT.

His peroration upon this subject is as follows: "The sum of all this is, there are in every person, even after he is justified, two contrary principles, nature and grace, termed by St. Paul, the flesh and the spirit; hence, although even babes in Christ are sanctified, yet it is only in part; in a degree, according to the measure of their faith, they are spiritual; yet in a degree they are carnal."

The doctrine indicated by the passage, "The spirit lusteth against the flesh, and the flesh against the spirit," is contained in Paul's letter to the Galatians, but instead of teaching Mr. Wesley's idea, presents the contrast between Judaism and Christianity. Hence says the apostle, "I am afraid of you, lest I have bestowed upon you labor in vain;" "Whosoever of you are justified by the law, ye are fallen from grace;" "O! foolish Galatians, who hath bewitched you, that ye should not obey the truth?"

"This only would I learn of you, received ye the spirit by the works of the law, or by the hearing of faith? Having began in the spirit, are ye now made perfect by the flesh? How turn ye again to the weak and beggarly elements, whereunto ye desire again to be in bondage?"

"Where is the blessedness ye spake of, for I bear you record, that if it had been possible, you would have plucked out your own eyes, and have given them to me. Have I become your enemy because I tell you the truth? My little children of whom I travail in birth again until Christ be formed in you, I desire to be present with you now, and to change my voice, for I stand in doubt of you. Tell me ye that desire to be under the law, do ye not hear the law? For it is written, that Abraham had two sons, the one by a bond-maid, the other by a free woman, but he who was of the bond-woman was born after the flesh; and he of the free woman was by promise, which things are an allegory; for these are the two covenants, the one from Mount Sinai, which gendereth to bondage, which is Haga, for this Haga is Mount Sinai in Arabia, and answereth to Jerusalem, which now is, and is in bondage with her children; but Jerusalem which is above, is free, which is the mother of us all. Now, we brethren, as Isaac was, are the children of promise, but as then, he that was born after the *flesh*, persecuted him that was born of the spirit, even so it is now. Nevertheless, what saith the Scriptures: Cast out the bond-woman and her son; for the son of the bond-woman shall not be heir with the son of the free woman.

"So, then, brethren, we are not the children of the bond-woman, but of the free; stand fast, therefore, in the liberty wherewith Christ hath made us free, and be not entangled again in the yoke of bondage; for brethren, ye have been called unto liberty, only use not liberty for an occasion to the flesh, but by love serve one another, for all the law is fulfilled in one word, even in this: Thou shalt love thy neighbor as thyself; but if ye bite and devour one another, take heed that ye be not consumed one of another.

"This I say, then, walk in the spirit, and ye shall not fulfill the lust of the flesh, for the flesh lusteth against the spirit, and the spirit against the flesh; and these are contrary, the one to the other, so that ye cannot do the things that ye would, for if ye be led by the spirit, ye are not under the law." *Rom.* viii: "There is, therefore, now no condemnation to them which are in Christ Jesus, who walk not after the flesh but after the spirit, for they that are in the flesh do mind the things of the flesh, but they that are after the spirit, the things of the spirit; for to be carnally minded is death, but to be spiritually minded is life and peace, because the carnal mind is enmity against God; for it is not subject to the law of God, neither indeed can be; so then they that are in the flesh cannot please God; but ye are not in the flesh, but in the spirit; therefore, brethren, we are debtors, not to the flesh, to live after the flesh, for if ye live after the flesh ye shall die."

In his letter to the Galatians, the apostle describes the fruits of Judaism, and those of Christianity the fruits of the spirit, and contrasts them thus: "Now the works of the flesh are manifest; which are these: Adultery, fornication, uncleanness, lasciviousness, idolatry, witchcraft, hatred, variance, emulations, wrath, strife, seditions, heresies, envyings, murders, drunkenness, revelings, and such like, of the which, I tell you, as I have told you in time past, that they which do such things shall not inherit the kingdom of God. But the fruit of the spirit is love, joy, peace, long suffering, gentleness, goodness, faith, meekness, temperance; against such there is no law, and they that are Christ's have crucified the flesh with the affections and lusts."

From these passages can anything be more evident than that those who are here described as being in the flesh, walking in the flesh, lusting after the flesh, and bearing the fruits of the flesh, who cannot please God, and who, therefore, shall die, are either Jews or backslidden Christians, who again desired to be under the law of Moses? And even if Christians are here meant, who lust after the flesh, which cannot be true, for Paul says, "ye brethren are not after the flesh," still it affords no proof in support of Mr. Wesley's doctrine, that such is the condition of the heart of all justified believers, and that, too, from the moment of their justification, because the apostle charges these as being in a backslidden state, with "having so soon departed from the gospel of Christ;" with having begun in the spirit, but desiring to be made perfect by the flesh (the law), they had become "bewitched," and had "fallen from grace;" thus had they become babes, and had lost their new birth condition, and with whom the apostle was under the necessity of again travailing with them in birth, till Christ should *again* be formed within them.

How preposterous that these backsliders, whose hearts now lusted against the spirit of Christ, who had turned again to the weak and beggarly elements (the law which had been the schoolmaster to bring them to Christ), under whose bondage they again desired to be, and to whom, in consequence, "Christ had become of none effect." We say that to hold up such as examples, illustrative of the hearts of all justified believers, is simply preposterous.

We have now shown that all the passages and expressions of Scripture which Mr. Wesley adduces in defence of his doctrine of sin in believers, utterly fails of accomplishing that purpose. Indeed, there is not a passage in the whole Bible in which God, Christ, the Holy Ghost or the apostles, utters any complaint, or finds the least fault with any saint who had preserved his Christian character as pure as it was when God first received him, and who had not committed actual transgression after his conversion.

Neither is it once said that there remained in any such heart the least sin of any kind, at the time of such reception or conversion; and is it possible a doctrine can be true which is not taught positively in a single text; and depends wholly upon inference, the unjustifiableness of which we have clearly seen? In addition to this, we hold there is not a passage in which the standard of Christian purity is held up, but that it is the condition of the heart, when it came first from the recreative hand of God, who never did anything imperfect. Its language is, "Where is the *blessedness* ye speak of?" Paul does not tell them that their hearts had been bad from the first, only they did not know it, and that they should have gone on from that point, and obtained the second blessing; then and not till then, would their hearts have been cleansed from all filthiness of the flesh; not a word of this is heard; but on the contrary, they had become again entangled with the yoke of bondage; again had they become contaminated by falling from their original state of gracious blessedness.

This passage describing the hearts of those who lusted against the spirit, and the spirit against the flesh, showing the two contrary principles in the hearts of all mere justified believers, as Mr. Wesley construes it, is the strongest one upon which he depends for the defence of his theory; but as we have seen, it describes those who were declared by the apostle to have fallen from grace, and hence the wickedness of those hearts; it utterly fails to furnish the least proof of his doctrine, neither does it furnish any for the idea that such feelings and desires can be in the heart of any Christian for a moment, and he be just in the sight of God. That a heart can be justified or just in the estimation of God, and yet lust against Christ, is simply blasphemy.

The fault God found with the church of Ephesus, was not that they had not progressed in holiness and purity and became more so from the time of their conversion, but on the contrary that they had left their first love; this was the standard therefore to which they were required to return: "repent, and do the first works over again." If they had these sins in their heart, it remained for Mr. Wesley to discover and teach that they were justified believers, and as such were sure of heaven.

That sin can be in the heart, and not manifest itself in words and acts, is not only contrary to its nature, but also to the philosophy as clearly taught by Christ concerning it.

Mat. vii, 16–20: "Ye shall know them by their fruits; do men gather grapes of thorns, or figs of thistles? even so every good tree bringeth forth good fruit, and a corrupt tree bringeth forth evil fruit; a good tree can not bring forth evil fruit; neither can a corrupt tree bring forth good fruit. Every tree that bringeth not forth good fruit, is hewn down, and cast into the fire. Wherefore by their fruits ye shall know them." Chapter xii, 33-35: "Either make the tree good, and his fruit good, or else make the tree corrupt and his fruit corrupt; for the tree is known by his fruit. O generation of vipers, how can ye, being evil, speak good things? For out of the abundance of the heart the mouth speaketh."

"A good man out of the good treasure of his heart bringeth forth good things; but an evil man out of the evil treasure bringeth forth evil things." *James* iii, 11, 12: "Doth a fountain send forth at the same place sweet water and bitter? Can a fig tree, my brethren, bear olive berries? Either a vine figs? So can no fountain both yield salt water and fresh."

In these concurrent passages we have the unmistakable doctrines taught, that what a man is in heart he will be in life; if his heart is corrupt, it will necessarily bring forth corrupt fruit, as surely as that a bitter fountain will taint all the waters flowing from it. The degree of bitterness in the fountain in order to produce this result does not come into the illustration; but as in nature, so in grace, the least degree of bitterness in the fountain taints all the waters flowing from it, teaching that the heart cannot be corrupt, in the least degree, and not manifest that corruption in corresponding words and actions; hence sin or depravity can not be in the heart of a justified believer. Neither can the heart be both corrupt and pure at the same time, part of each. "Doth a fountain send forth bitter and sweet water at the same place?" "Therefore, make the heart good (not a part of it), and the fruit will be good." Can Jesus leave a sinner's heart, which he has promised to make new, partly corrupt, unless he belies his own gospel as here set forth? These are teachings coming from the great master himself, with which the idea is utterly irreconcilable, that a heart can be partly pure and partly impure at the same time, and especially that it can be such when Jesus first translates it into the kingdom.

The only way in which a heart can become corrupt after being once purified, is illustrated by Christ in the same chapter, thus: "When the unclean spirit is gone out of a man, he (the unclean spirit) walketh through dry places seeking rest, and findeth none." Then he saith, "I will return into my house, from whence I came out, and when he is come he findeth it empty, swept and garnished (he did not find any filthiness of the flesh or spirit there), then goeth he, and taketh with him seven other spirits more wicked than himself, and they enter in and dwell there; and the last state of that man is worse than the first."

This is further illustrated in the 28th and 29th verses: "But if I cast out devils by the spirit of God, then the kingdom of God is come unto you, or else how can one enter into a strong man's house and spoil his goods, except he first bind the strong man, and then he will spoil his house?" According to the doctrine, that a part of all sin (the goods of Satan) remains in the hearts of all believers from the moment of their conversion, Christ should have said it is true, I enter into the house "where satan dwelleth," and bind him with chains, but do not cast him out, although I have taught that "I cast out devils by the spirit of God," I leave him to occupy one corner, and I take up my abode in the other; and the sentiment, "how can two walk together except they be agreed," is false. I have power to cast out satan by the spirit of God, proving that the kingdom of God is come, for surely if I can bind him in fetters I can do the easier work of casting him out, and if it is morally consistent for me to bind the strong man, it must be also to cast him out; but I have too much respect for satan and his goods to deal thus harshly, and I have but little respect for the house itself; this I do not empty of sin, satan's goods, nor sweep nor garnish it; I leave it partly unsanctified and filthy. The binding of satan and the spoiling of his goods, means preserving some of them, and only keeping the others down for a time at least, and thus I deceive the man, in leaving him to suppose they are all destroyed and the house garnished. I will in a little time let loose the whole troop, and so far unchain them that they will make a dreadful stir in the house, and a horrid warfare will again commence where all was peace. I have no particular object in this, and some are even ruined by it, but such is my policy, though it is positively contrary to my revealed word. The deaf and dumb devil whom I have just cast out, and which event called out the sayings regarding the casting out of satan, the spoliation of his goods, and the garnishing the house wherein he dwelt, was a perfect cure. I did not leave the man deaf in one ear, or partly so in both, nor partly dumb, which I should have done if I intended to teach the doctrine of sin in all believers' hearts from the time I attempt to effect a moral cure.

We turn from this dreadful picture, this monstrous sentiment, relieved to know that from our Lord came no such word or act; he never cured a man, in whom he did not immediately effect a perfect cure, and he never changed the heart of a sinner, but it was a perfect change. If he gives a new heart, it is no patch on the old garment; he never puts the new wine of the kingdom into other than new bottles; he makes the tree *good*, and the good fruit grows naturally thereon; he cleanses the bitter from the fountain, and from it flows naturally the sweet water.

We assume here, that it is the normal condition of man to be thus in harmony and fellowship with God. The introduction of sin into the world philosophically and scripturally, accounts for the existing estrangement and moral antagonism between man and his maker, which the gospel alone has power to remedy. It, therefore, originated with the God of creation. We propose here to show what is meant by loving God with all the heart.

In order to do this, one of two things is necessary: First, to love God to the exclusion of every one else; or secondly, to love him supremely, or above everything or being else. That the first of these propositions cannot be true, is shown by the fact that in one of the great commandments, "upon which hang all the law and the prophets," God enjoins the solemn duty on those who love him with all the heart of loving their neighbors also. "Thou shalt love the Lord thy God with all thy heart, and thy neighbor as thyself." Therefore, it is certain that to love God with all the heart, is not to love him exclusively; and it follows that our second proposition—to love him supremely—must be correct.

This truth we find, like every other doctrine of the Bible, so beautifully, forcibly and perfectly presented by the great teacher himself, that leaves no room for honest doubt as to its signification. *Mat.* x, 37: "He that loveth father or mother more than me, is not worthy of me; and he that loveth son or daughter more than me is not worthy of me." There are other tests by which men may know whether they love God thus perfectly or supremely, or with all their heart; for on the authority of Jesus, we consider the position established that to love God with all the heart, is to love him supremely, nothing more or less.

One of these tests is, that those who thus love God, receive the teachings of Christ in preference to those of men, when there is disagreement; to such the sayings of Jesus, or his words, which were not his own, but the Father's, which sent him, are the standard of appeal in the settlement of all doctrines. "He that loveth me keepeth *my words,* and my Father will love him. He that hath my commandments and keepeth them, he it is that loveth me." To give a practical illustration, let us suppose a man investigates the arguments here presented, and becomes convinced that the doctrine taught by Jesus and the apostles is, that no sin remains in the heart of justified believers at and after their conversion, unless they backslide. Now, notwithstanding this, the man still determines to adhere to the theory of Mr. Wesley to the contrary, can such a man be said to receive the words of Christ and believe them in preference to those of Wesley? and as men are sanctified and kept pure by the belief of those words, "sanctify them through thy truth," "now ye are clean through the words which I have spoken unto you," can they be clean or sanctified by the disbelief and rejection of those words? which they do by receiving those of men as entitled to the greatest authority.

It is no wonder such a heart has in it all the sins which Mr. Wesley, unfortunately, makes the inbred inheritance of all mere justified believers. No marvel that such a heart, in its bigotry, which is the result of its education received since conversion, has the carnal mind, and a "spirit lusting against Christ," enmity against God, manifestly in a state of subjection to the opinions of men, and not subject to the law (or words) of God. His heart revolts at the teachings of Jesus; he hates them by prefering those of men, or his own preconceived opinions, if he ever dare entertain any, which he did not receive from his standard authors. Question these, and his spirit rises up to crush the opposition, though it comes armed "with the whole panoply of God;" he calls to his aid, if he have the influence and power, church excommunications, and the anti-Christian spirit of persecution.

Those whose arguments he is utterly unable to meet, he adopts the easier course, and denounces them as heretics; they must be "rebuked," he cries. That Satan, after having been once exorcised, has again entered such a heart and mind, there can be no question. In his first love he had none of this bitter spirit; he then received the words of Jesus as truth which he could easily understand, but he has had another education, and a sectarian one since, hence his spirit and his words, like the Galatians, he has become bewitched by error. But thank God the day is past when such efforts can crush the truth; intelligent Christianity appeals now to the highest authority, and the man who appeals to commentators, even in Sabbath school Bible classes, becomes the subject of severe criticism. "What saith the Scriptures?" is the inquiry. To attempt, therefore, to crush out this intelligent and independent thought of the age, is to engender skepticism and infidelity, and cannot succeed; and all such efforts coming from whatever source, only exhibits the weakness and ignorance of those who exemplify them. He who dares not think for himself is a mere servile slave to the opinions of others, and should have been born in the tenth century. It needs no proof that such do not love God with all their heart, and yet it is this very class, more than any other, who make this exclusive profession of reverence for human opinion. If we appeal to the Bible, it is just as easy to show that all young converts love God with all their heart, as that they love him at all.

To determine this, John furnishes us with another test, that of fear: "There is no fear in love; he that feareth is not made perfect in love; fear hath torment." From these words it is clear that those who have been delivered from tormenting fear have been made perfect in love; and was it ever known that a newly converted child of God had *tormenting fear?* Indeed, was it ever known that any Christian, unless he had become a willful transgressor of the authority of God, had tormenting fear, and felt that it would be a fearful thing for him to "fall into the hands of the living God?" "Fear hath torment, but perfect love casteth out all fear," hence every Christian who has not backslidden, and who has no tormenting fear, has perfect love, and loves God with all his heart; but no man can say this if he has left his first love, and has not repented and done the first works over again. No man can say he loves God with all his heart who has ceased to abide in Christ, and to walk in him as he received him, unless he has "returned again to the shepherd and bishop of his soul," and by his blood been again cleansed from the effects of his apostacy. Jesus said to him: "Now ye are clean through the words which I have spoken unto you," but he wandered, and has come back, and is again purified as at first. "He has now been delivered from an evil heart of unbelief in departing from the living God," showing that this evil heart was the result of the departing from God, or of leaving his first love, and is not, as Mr. Wesley contends, the normal condition of the heart of all merely justified believers.

Mr. Wesley attributes the doctrine, that Jesus cleanses the hearts of all whom he receives from all sin, to Count Zinzendorf, and says "it is attended with the most fatal consequences, because it cuts off all watching against an evil heart of unbelief; the Delilah, which we are told, is gone, though she is still lying in our bosom."

This superficial and sophisticated reasoning is only exceptional with Mr. Wesley, whose critical perception and logical mind generally leaves a position assumed clearly established, if, indeed, not unanswerable; and this exception only proves the erroneous character of the sentiment he is advocating. For instance, how can a man watch against an attack from an enemy he possesses in his heart, and which would not be there only as he desires his retention, and when found there, the only remedy for its destruction is in the blood of Christ. It is the duty of the man to see and feel it if it exists, and by instant prayer and faith apply to the blood of atonement to have it washed away.

The idea of turning the sacred duty of Christian watchfulness to the taming or modification of the Delilah, or the viper sin in our bosom, to see that she is well bound, but keeping her still in the heart as a harmless pet where Jesus should reign alone, presents one of the most fanciful absurdities conceivable.

The only course God appoints for a sinner or a backslidden saint, is to take the Delilahs by earnest repentance and faith to Jesus, to have him cast them out. Let him again sweep the house empty, and garnish it, and thus restore it to be a fit temple of the Holy Ghost.

Mr. Wesley well says in another place: "When a man makes this discovery of sin in his heart, unless he pursues this course, he can go no further;" and according to Jesus, he cannot stand still, "for he that gathereth not with me, scattereth abroad;" and hence he must go further back still, or become again cleansed. It is not, therefore, the duty of a man, with an unsanctified heart to watch against that, but it is the duty of the man out of whose heart Christ has cast the devil, and spoiled his goods, leaving it clean, swept and garnished, to stand on perpetual watch to resist the first onset of the devil when he returns with his reinforcement of seven other spirits more wicked than himself, lest he and them enter there again and dwell, making the last state of that man worse than the first."

The appropriate position for a man who has this enemy chained in his heart, is to open wide the door, unloose his chains, and watch anxiously his escape.

What would be thought of a jailer who had a troublesome prisoner, unlawfully held, and earnestly wishing his escape, who nevertheless should go into his cell, put a chain on every limb, fasten them firmly to the floor, lock and bar the doors and grates, and then, through a crevice, watch for his escape?

Instead of the doctrine for which we contend, being dangerous and fatal, we hold that such is the doctrine of Mr. Wesley. Here is a man, for instance, who has a carnal mind that makes him "love all evil," and such a heart, according to Mr. Wesley, is that of every justified believer, and that, too, from the very moment of his conversion, and as a justified believer he is sure of heaven. What can be a more fatal deception? But we argue that if "the love of all evil" is in a converted soul, that soul must know it, because it is a feeling: that of love, "the love of all evil," and is it not impossible to love a thing or being, and not know it?

According to Mr. Wesley's admission, that no love is felt for evil in the heart when first converted there can none exist.

CHAPTER IX.

TEE SMALLEST DEGREE OF FAITH SAVES THE SOUL

The assumption that all justified believers have a proneness to, and love for all evil, and are carnally minded, besides the abstract manner in which these expressions, descriptive of sin in believers, are calculated to deceive those who have no such hearts, simply by their ambiguity. One of those commonly used in this connection, is that of "the roots of bitterness."

We may just remark here, that it is apparent to all who have examined this subject, that the most difficult feature with which its advocates have to contend, is the want of terms to describe the moral condition of a heart which is justified but not sanctified. They need terms which will describe a heart, to be at the same time both clean and unclean; that loves and hates the same object; that is innocent and guilty; that needs to repent of what another done (for Adam's sin which they have in their heart), to be perfect and imperfect, righteous and unrighteous, holy and unholy, pure and impure, just in the sight of God, and not just, a believing and unbelieving heart, sanctified and unsanctified.

Now this very incongruity, this necessity of terms meaning opposites, and there being no such, demonstrates the idea attempted to be taught, a most foolish and absurd error.

As there is no other way of understanding the meaning of Scripture terms only by examining the passages in which they occur, and hence to obtain the proper definition, and as it is generally to erroneous definitions of terms, this, and all other errors are to be attributed, it is the only course by which we can arrive at truth.

The expression above alluded to, is found in *Heb.* xii, 12, 16: " Wherefore lift up the hands which hang down, and the feeble knees; and make straight paths for your feet, lest that which is lame be turned out of the way, but rather let it be healed, follow peace with all men and holiness, without which no man shall see the Lord; looking diligently lest any man fail of the grace of God, lest any root of bitterness springing up trouble you, and thereby many be defiled, lest there be any fornicator or profane person, as Esau, who for one morsel of meat sold his birthright."

The roots of bitterness springing up, against which these Christians were warned, meant sinful acts, as fornicators or profane persons, "whereby many were defiled, and thereby had fallen from the grace of God." Already their hands had hung down, and their knees were feeble, instead of walking firmly and steadily in the narrow way. Already they had made crooked paths for their feet, instead of obeying the instruction, "Make straight paths for your feet," and had become lame by walking therein, and were cautioned against being turned entirely out of the way, and enjoined rather to let their moral lameness be healed. The purity from which they had wandered, was held up as the standard which alone gives peace and holiness, and qualifies for the service of God. Such should remember the fate of Esau, who by his profanity fell so far that he found no place of repentance, though he sought it earnestly with tears.

Such a course and result is indeed a root of bitterness, but who cannot see that it has no reference whatever to remaining sin in the hearts of justified saints from the time of their conversion, and, therefore, furnishes no proof of Mr. Wesley's doctrine.

In regard to unbelief in believers, he says: "The word has two meanings, either little faith or no faith; the absence of faith, or its weakness. In the former sense unbelief is commonly mixed with a doubt or fear, that is, in the latter sense with unbelief. Why are ye fearful, says our Lord, O! ye of little faith. Again: O! thou of little faith, wherefore didst thou doubt? You see, here was unbelief in believers." In proof of this plausible argument, Mr. Wesley introduces two passages of Scripture, and we shall see that neither of them teaches his sentiment.

In the first place, we remark that the Bible clearly discriminates between the "faith that worketh by love and purifieth the heart," as it is expressed, and the faith to work miracles, and we shall see that these two passages refer to the latter faith.

That the faith to work miracles may exist in the absence of that which makes a man's heart Christ-like, is clearly taught by Paul. 1 *Cor.* xiii, 2: "And though I have *all have*, so that I could remove mountains, and have not charity, I am nothing."

That the word charity here comprehends the whole spirit of the gospel, is evident from what it does. "It suffereth long, is kind, envieth not, vaunteth not itself, is not puffed up, seeketh not her own, is not easily provoked, thinketh no evil, rejoiceth, not in iniquity, but rejoiceth in the truth, believeth all things, endureth all things." Here we see that a man may have all faith to work miracles, and yet not have charity, and "charity believeth all things," and therefore, includes the faith which transforms the heart into the image of God. That the expression, "O! ye of little faith," was the faith which enables to work miracles, is clearly seen by its connection.

Matt. xiv, 28-31: "And Peter said, Lord if it be thou, bid me come unto thee on the water, and he said come, and Peter walked on the water to go to Jesus, but when he saw the wind boisterous, he was afraid; and beginning to sink, he cried out, saying Lord save me, and immediately Jesus stretched forth his hand, and caught him, and said unto him, O! ye of little faith, wherefore didst thou doubt?"

The term little faith here, means that Peter had no faith adequate to work this miracle of setting aside the laws of gravitation and of atmospheric pressure, in regard to which Jesus taught that the smallest degree of faith was all that was demanded to work the greatest miracle. *Matt.* xvii, 19, 20: "Then came the disciples to Jesus apart, and said, Why could not we cast him out? And Jesus said unto them, because of your unbelief; for verily I say unto you, if ye have faith as a grain of mustard seed, which is less than all the seeds that be in the earth, ye shall say unto this mountain, remove hence to yonder place, and it shall remove; and nothing shall be impossible to you."

If Peter, therefore, had possessed as small a degree of faith as this, and the legitimate teaching of the figure is that it is the very smallest, on this occasion, he could have walked on the sea safely to Jesus, but he was as faithless to accomplish this feat as were these disciples to cast out this devil, and therefore they both failed.

In the record Mark gives of this transaction, it is positively declared that the disciples on the ship, amid the storm, had no faith to quell it. "And Jesus arose and rebuked the wind, and said unto the sea, peace, be still, and the wind ceased, and there was a great calm; and he said unto them: Why are ye so fearful? How is it that ye have *no faith?*"

Is it not conclusive from these passages, when properly understood, that they do not teach what Mr. Wesley endeavors to make them—that is, that saving faith in Jesus and damning unbelief exists in the same heart, and in the hearts of all mere justified believers.

The disciples certainly had not apostatized from having saving faith in Jesus, and yet he declares they had *no faith*, from which we conclude that a man may have the faith in Jesus "which works by love and purifies the heart," and not have the least faith to work miracles; and as these passages relate to the faith to work miracles, and not to that which purifies the heart, in which latter sense Mr. Wesley uses them, he utterly fails of his purpose, and with all others must forever fail in such an attempt, from the fact that the Bible teaches no such doctrine.

We would not even appear to cast the least reflection upon a man of such intelligence and godly attainments as the sainted Wesley; and what astonishes us most is, that he should have seen and taught so much truth, taking into consideration the floods of error the reformers brought out of Papacy, with which he was surrounded, and the moral darkness of the Protestant church at that period, and to say he was not vastly in advance of his age, would be to contradict history. But in his attempt to establish the doctrine of the second blessing, and consequently of sin in believers, as the grounds for it, he fails in every point to distinguish or to accept the distinction, that there were in all the churches and in all periods three classes of professors: First, those who had always maintained their integrity and purity from their conversion, such as those thus addressed: "I have a few names even in Sardis who have not defiled their garments, and they shall walk with me in white, for they are worthy." Secondly, those who had left their first love and become again contaminated by the filthiness of sin; "who had evil hearts of unbelief in departing from the living God," the very departing begetting the evil heart. Here, by the way, is the philosophy or theology of sin in believers; they were once such, but now unbelievers, because a man cannot be a believer and be departing from the living God at the same time. Thirdly, those who, from various motives and under various delusions, have found their way into the church, who were never converted at all, and thus we find that there was not an epistle wrote to any of the apostolic churches in which, at least, two of these classes, and generally the third, were not recognized.

It is because Mr. Wesley did not appreciate or acknowledge this fact that led him into error in regard to this subject. Some walked in the spirit, as they had commenced; others fell from this grace and became again entangled and contaminated by the filthiness of the flesh, and some "hated even the garments spotted by the flesh;" some preserved their spiritual mindedness, while others, in the same church, had become carnally minded. To these several classes were the epistles, as well as the angelic messages to the seven churches of Asia, addressed.

In order for Mr. Wesley to make out his doctrine of sin in believers, he selects the class who had fallen from their original state of purity as the example, instead of that of the class who had always remained pure, and holds up their condition of heart and life as that of all justified believers, and therefore erroneously concludes that there is a part of all sin left in the heart of all believers at and from the moment of their justification.

As the least degree of the faith to work miracles enables its possessor to work the greatest, we have a right to infer that the least degree of faith in Jesus gives purity of heart; we mean perfect purity, and indeed this qualification is superfluous, because that which is not perfectly pure is positively impure; and unless the heart can be divided, so that a part may be pure and a part impure, it must be either wholly pure or wholly impure. It is unquestionably true that there is strong and weak faith—we mean saving faith, or "that which works by love and purifies the heart" (this being Paul's definition, we like it best)—but upon this point Mr. Wesley commits another error, in concluding that where there is little faith there is much unbelief, as though every mind had just such a quantity of belief and unbelief, and in the same ratio in which one diminishes the other increases — entirely ignoring the simplest and most universally conceded thought God ever revealed to man, which is that the whole human race, at least who hear the gospel, are divided in their relations to him into two and only two classes, and the great principle of that classification is belief and unbelief, the consequences of either and both are thus emphatically pronounced: "He that believeth shall be saved, and he that believeth not shall be damned."

If a man could be a believer and an unbeliever, or have some faith and some unbelief (which is the same thing) at the same time, he would belong to both of these classes, or to neither. The consequence would be that God could do nothing with him, as it respects future rewards and punishments, only on the supposition of dividing the man, saving the believing part and damning the unbelieving part.

The only principle we can conceive, upon which impartial justice can be done to sinners, is that the smallest degree of faith in Christ saves from sin, and saves in heaven, because there are, owing to the limitation of mental calibre and cultivation and the shortness of human life and the suddenness of death, those who could not otherwise be saved, while on the other hand, the smallest degree of unbelief against Christ, is damning in its nature; and if it could be in the heart of a Christian, which we hold to be impossible, would be the more deserving of damnation than in the heart of a sinner who was never converted, because the sin of the unbelief of the Christian is against the greater light.

If, therefore, a man is a believer at all, and has the smallest degree of faith in Jesus, he obtains pardon from all his guilt, and purity from all his depravity, together with a title to life and immortality, and the greatest degree of faith gives its possessor no greater pardon, purity or salvation. "It is required of a man according to that which he hath, and not according to that which he hath not:" "Where much is given, much is required, and where little is given, little is required."

Therefore, as far as it respects the pardon, purity and salvation of sinners, every man who has any faith at all to be saved, receives the same, and receives it all.

If any man is dissatisfied at such a gracious distribution, supposing he, in his self-conceit, should be elevated to a more conspicuous position than his not so fortunate neighbor, and in consideration of the great advantage he has been to God and his cause, that something should be said or done to give him distinction in the other world.

In regard to such, we venture the remark, that unless pride and selfishness enter into the kingdom of God, the man with such feelings and aspirations will never gain an inheritance among those whose chief characteristic will be that of humility. Besides, we will copy for the benefit of such the instruction given in advance, and applicable to the case.

Matt. 20: "For the kingdom of heaven is like unto a man that is a householder, which went out early in the morning to hire laborers into his vineyard, and when he had agreed with the laborers for a penny a day, he sent them into his vineyard. And he went out about the third hour, and saw others standing idle in the market place, and said unto them, go ye also into the vineyard, and whatsoever is right I will give you. Again he went out about the sixth and ninth hours, and did likewise. And about the eleventh hour, he went out and found others standing idle, and saith unto them, why stand ye here all the day idle? and they say unto him, because no man hath hired us; he saith unto them, go ye also into the vineyard, and whatsoever is right, that shall ye receive. So when even was come, the lord of the vineyard saith unto his steward, call the laborers and give them their hire, beginning from the last unto the first. And when they came that was hired about the eleventh hour, they received every man a penny; but when the first came, they supposed that they should have received more, and they likewise received every man a penny, and when they had received it, they murmured against the good man of the house, saying, these last have wrought but one hour, and thou hast made them equal unto us, which have borne the burden and heat of the day; but he answered one of them and said: Friend, I do thee no wrong; didst thou not agree with me for a penny? Take that thine is, and go thy way; I will give unto this last even as unto thee; is it not lawful for me to do what I will with my own? Is thine eye evil because mine is good?"

We apprehend that those who are so fortunate as to enter the kingdom of God, not only the first impulse will be a marvel how they got there at all, but a theme of eternal wonder that God

> "Should make slaves the partners of his throne,
> Decked with a never-fading crown."

If we should suppose a case who had what we deem the smallest degree of faith in Christ to be saved from sin, it would be the following: *Mat.* ix, 2: "And behold, they brought to him a man sick of palsy, lying on a bed, and Jesus, seeing their faith, said unto the sick of the palsy: Son, be of good cheer, thy sins be forgiven thee. And behold, certain of the Scribes said within themselves, this man blasphemeth; and Jesus, knowing their thoughts, said: Wherefore think ye evil in your hearts, for whether is easier to say, thy sins be forgiven thee, or to say, arise and walk? But that ye may know that the Son of man hath power on earth to forgive sins, then saith he to the sick of the palsy, arise, take up thy bed, and go unto thy house, and he arose and departed unto his house."

Here we have a man whose friends had faith that Jesus could cure his palsy, and for this purpose they brought him. In honor of that faith, Jesus not only cured his sickness, but pardoned his sins; and there is not the least evidence that in the faith of his friends, even, there was any thought or conception of Jesus forgiving the man's sins, and if he himself had any such faith, Jesus would have recognized it. Now, as it was consistent for him to cure the man's palsy on the strength of the faith of others, so was it also to forgive his sins, though not an intimation had been made or entertained, either by the sick man or his friends, relating to it, yet such was the sequel. But as it is not possible for Jesus to forgive sins without faith, this man must have had some faith in the power of Christ, not only to heal his disease, but to do for him whatever he needed, although he had no distinct conception of what it was; and therefore while healing his palsy, Jesus done for him what was infinitely more important, and was all he needed, pardoned his sins.

We have already seen that Jesus announced the principle that if it was consistent for him to cleanse a sinner at all, he could and would completely cleanse him from all sin. "If I wash thee not," said he to Peter, "thou hast no part in me." "Then," said Peter, "not my feet alone, but my hands and my head." But Jesus said unto him: "He that is washed needeth not save to wash his feet, but is clean every whit."

Is it not the conclusion from these teachings that if a man has the least conceivable degree of faith in Jesus, so that he can do anything in any manner for him, that he can do all he needs, and that he will do it; if he heals his palsy he forgives his sins, although he does not ask or think about this. If he forgives his sins, so as to give the sinner a part in him, he cleanses his heart from moral corruption; and if he cleanses it at all, he makes it "clean every whit." If this is not the teaching of him who spake as never man spake, in vain may man endeavor to understand anything he taught. But it is said: "Faith is the gift of God." Suppose it is, so is eternal life; but there are conditions upon which the bestowment is made, and which must be consistent with God's government.

Paul says: "Faith cometh by hearing, and hearing by the word of God;" hence the man who takes most heed as to how he hears, as "new born babes desire the sincere milk of the word, that they may grow thereby," make the most rapid progress, and consequently have the greatest degree of evidence upon which faith is founded, and therefore have the greatest degree of faith, and of course he who hears and receives least of the teachings of the word of God, to him cometh the least degree of faith, because "faith cometh by hearing, and hearing by the word of God;" hence the command: "Go ye into all the world and preach the gospel to every creature. He that believeth shall be saved; he that believeth not, shall be damned." According to this, there are as many degrees of faith as there are individuals who hear and receive the word of God, hence the expressions, strong and weak faith; but the weak faith in the true penitent, just coming to Jesus, seeking him as the object of his love, crying, "where is he whom my soul loveth," works by love and purifies the heart, just as perfectly as does the strongest; and it is no more true "that without faith it is impossible to please God," than that those having the least faith do please him. And it is also no more true that those who grow most rapidly in grace, and in the knowlege of the truth, as it is in Jesus, or as taught by Jesus, have the strongest faith, than that those whose circumstances admit only of more moderate progress in this knowledge, are just as pure as the others. That the one with the five talents is no more pure, or more pleasingly meets God's approbation in time and eternity, than the one having the two.

Dr. Young thus beautifully puts this truth into poetry:

> He that does the best his circumstances admit,
> Does well, acts nobly; angels can do no more.

The fact is, the degree of faith or intelligence, if it is removed above blank idiocy, has no connection whatever with the degree of Christian purity; it has with the degree of steadiness and constancy of Christian character, makes a man a pillar in the church. It was the strength of Abraham's faith which moved God to call him the "Father of the faithful."

It is by confounding the degree of purity with the degree of faith, which led Mr. Wesley and all who advocate his doctrine of sin in believers, to commit another error, and who must forever be involved in it, unless they become humble enough to pluck out these right eyes of preconceived opinion, and go directly to Jesus and the apostles for truth. Then, indeed, will they be sanctified by its belief, and not till then. Then, indeed, will they be "chosen through sanctification of the spirit and belief of the truth." Then, indeed, will they be clean through the words which Jesus has spoken unto them.

This will be a sanctification which is "not puffed up, vaunteth not itself, and doth not behave itself unseemly," by parading its high attainments before others. It will be a purity appearing most conspicuously in its humility, esteeming others better than themselves, instead of themselves better than others, as these modern second blessing professors generally do. Such will find it wholly unnecessary to profess to be anything but Christians. They will have such views of Christ as they draw near and behold him as "the sun shining in his strength," that their only embarrassment will be in making such an exalted profession, as being his follower, by living within the circle of his glowing light, they will behold such a contrast, that with the holy prophet they will cry out, " Woe is me, for I am undone; because I am a man of unclean lips, and I dwell in the midst of a people of unclean lips, for mine eyes have seen the king, the Lord of hosts."

CHAPTER X.

THE DANGER OF THIS DOCTRINE.

The evil tendency and dangerous results of this erroneous doctrine, is in deluding formal professors and backsliders into the belief that although they have all these sins in their hearts, they are, nevertheless, justified believers, and as such, are sure of heaven; thereby encouraging them to continue in such a state of heart, of which there are thousands in the church.

There are also others who have never been converted, some of whom under religious excitement, when mere children, joined the church, and if they became converted afterwards, while perhaps engaged in seeking the second blessing, but which is really only the first, and it is this class who draw comparisons between the first and second blessing, and make the first but a few drops in comparison with the ocean of the second, when the fact is, they never had the first at all; if they had, they could never belittle it in this way; but here is one of the delusions of this doctrine; error is always fruitful.

But we say that when backsliders and those never converted, hear the second blessing doctrine, describing such a state of heart as Mr. Wesley declares that to be of all mere justified believers, they feel and know that their hearts are no worse than the picture, and are therefore, encouraged to continue in this state of heart.

Besides this, there is the dreadful influence produced by such teaching, that the justification of sinners is but a very little thing, because it leaves men with such bad hearts, all filthy, corrupt, depraved, unclean, impure and unholy as to be "in love with all evil," as Mr. Wesley says of them. Such a change they feel, is not only unimportant, but hardly worth having; thus is God's great truth degraded, which the Bible represents to be the most wonderful work the great God ever performed. "That God can be just, and yet the justifier of him that believeth in Jesus." How God can still be a being of truth and veracity, and justify the sinful soul, when he had unqualifiedly declared "The soul that sinneth, it shall die." The fatal delusion of this doctrine is, that it cries peace and safety to those whose hearts have either become corrupt and sinful by ceasing to abide in Christ, or to those carnal minded professors, who are in the nominal church, but who were never in Christ at all.

Let it be proclaimed in the whole Protestant church, "Without holiness, no man shall see the Lord," and that if the heart of a Christian is unholy or unclean, it has become such if once converted, by "leaving its first love," holding up as the standard, the continual maintainence of sanctified hearts from conversion, and what a marvellous change would come over the whole church. The position we hold to be unanswerable, that no doctrine can be true, the tendency of which is to encourage any human being, who has any sin in his heart, to feel safe in his relation with God, even for a single moment. We object to the idea of universal salvation, from the fact that its legitimate tendency is to strengthen the wicked to continue such.

We also object to the idea of partial election

and the necessary perseverance of the saints, because it encourages those who were once converted, to be easy subjects of temptation, and to live loose lives by the perpetration of acts, which if they thought would endanger their salvation, they would never do.

But here in our church we have a worse deception than any of these, a doctrine which describes a heart in love with all evil, having carnal mindedness, pride, hatred, self will, unbelief, anger, envy, covetousness, jealousy, idolatry, lusting after the flesh, lovers of pleasure, more than lovers of God, as being the state of the hearts of all justified believers, and that, too, from the moment of their justification, and which holds, that as such, they are sure of being saved, if they die instantly.

We suppose such will only be undeceived, so strong is this delusion believed, when they find themselves among those who stand without, after the master of the house has risen up and shut to the door, crying, "Lord, Lord, open unto us," to whom the response will be, "Depart from me, ye workers of iniquity."

But Mr. Wesley also offers as proof of the

doctrine of the sinful hearts of all mere justified believers, the fact that it is the experience of so large a proportion of them.

In charity for Mr. Wesley's views upon this subject, we cannot but attribute it to his former views as an extreme formalist, we mean before he was taught the doctrine of justification, by faith alone, by the Moravians. It is the same thing, though not done intentionally, of "binding heavy burdens," those of the law, or seeking to be justified by the righteousness of the law, which is clearly the drift of Mr. Wesley's teachings in the following passage (Page 119, Sermon on Sin in Believers): "But let it be supposed that they (justified believers) continually watch and pray, and so do not enter into temptation; that they continually set a watch before their mouth, and keep the door of their lips. Suppose they exercise themselves herein, that all their conversation may be in grace, seasoned with salt, and meat to minister grace to the hearers; yet do they not daily slide into useless discourse, notwithstanding all their caution? and even when they endeavor to speak for God, are their words pure? Do they find nothing wrong in their very intention? Do they speak merely to please God, and not partly to please themselves? Is it wholly to do the will of God, and not their own will also? Or, if they begin with a single eye, do they go on looking unto Jesus, and talking with him all the time they are talking with their neighbors? When they are reproving sin, do they feel no anger or unkind temper at the sinner? When they are instructing the ignorant, do they not find any pride, any self-preference? When they are comforting the afflicted, or provoking one another to love and to good works, do they never feel inward commendation—now you have spoken well—or any vanity, as a desire that others should think so, and esteem them on that account? In some or all of these respects, how much sin cleaves to the *best conversation*, even of believers? The conviction of which is another branch of the repentance which belongs to believers."

In regard to this picture, it must be remembered it is that of justified believers, from which state of heart his second blessing doctrine, or sanctification, as he interprets it, proposes to deliver its recipients. If this be so, it is very certain there are none in our day in possession of this state. There is not a man on earth, nor ever was, who for a single day or hour, when he was not asleep or insane, who kept all these rules without infringement. It paints a picture of nothing less than angelic and absolute perfection, and taints the very best conversation of any mortal with sin, as nothing but absolute perfection can do; and it must be also remembered that the object for which the sermon was wrote was to combat a man who had preached in a certain place that God cleansed the heart when he justified a sinner, and made it pure; and in order to succeed, he draws this adroit and spurious description, as that of the hearts of all when first converted. But we hold that these rules or requirements are only obtained by a misapprehension and misconstruction of the expressions of Scripture here introduced, which will be apparent as we ask those questions again, and give such answers to them as we suppose the purest Christian ever lived may intelligently and conscientiously give. In answer to what is first said of Christians walking and being in grace, closing with the sentence: "And meat to minister grace to the hearers, yet do they not not daily slide into useless discourse, notwithstanding all their caution?" We answer emphatically *no*, because if they are born again, and do not backslide in heart, and if they do in heart, it will show itself in life, they fully meet all the requisitions of Christ's precepts, and those of the apostles: "He keepeth himself, and that wicked one toucheth him not."

But again: "When they endeavor to speak for God, are their words pure—free from unholy mixture?" We answer, yes; because *their endeavor* to do so, supposes purity of motive and intention, and this is perfect Christian purity itself, and there is nothing more of it. "First make the tree good, and the fruit will be good, for a good tree cannot produce evil fruit." (*Christ.*)

"Do they find nothing wrong in their intention?" We answer, no; and for the same reason. An endeavor to speak for God is an intention to thus speak; and we will add, that the idea implied in the question is nothing but an ambiguous endeavor to show the existence of sin in a heart where there is none; the tendency of which is to deceive the ignorant.

"Do they speak merely to please God, and not partly to please themselves?" Answer: They may do both, and be as innocent and pure as him who said: "*My delight* is in the law of the Lord." No man can please God, and endeavor to do so, without pleasing himself also. It involves a philosophic impossibility.

"Is it wholly to do the will of God, and not their own will also?" We answer: A man's will may be in such perfect harmony with God, and in subjection to his will, that the will of the one is that of the other. He may do this, and be as holy as him who said: "My meat and drink is to do the will of him that sent me." And this is holiness, or God-likeness, and it is all of it. A perfect saint may therefore do the will of God, and at the same time his own will also.

"If they begin with a single eye, do they

go on, looking unto Jesus?" Answer: If they do not, it is not to be attributed to sin chained in their hearts, but to such as the sin of the woman, who once looked back, for which God struck her into a pillar of salt; of whom Jesus said, to admonish such as should cease to look to him: "Remember Lot's wife."

"Do they talk with Jesus all the time they are talking with their neighbor?" Answer: The question involves absurdity.

"When they are reproving sin, do they feel no anger or unkind temper to the sinner?" Answer: There is no such thing, as the question seems to suppose, as sin abstract from the sinner; but as it is the act of the sinner, God and man holds him responsible, and if, by the words anger and temper, the same is meant, then we say that a perfect saint may be so highly excited against a godless and incorrigible sinner, that it reaches indignation; but it is holy indignation; and if it is as holy as God (which is simply God-likeness), such would be his feeling; for it is written: "God is angry with the wicked every day; and also: "Be ye angry and sin not."

"If they are instructing the ignorant, do they not find any pride and self-preference?" We answer: If they do, it is not latent or indwelling sin, chained in the heart, but the active work of pride, which it must be, in order to be pride, and in this case mixed with self-conceit; either of which savors more of the sin of Lucifer than of the humility of a Christian. That it may be determined whether men have self-preference while engaged in the instruction of the ignorant, it is only necessary to know whether they are teaching them their own opinions or the doctrines of mere men, in preference to the word of God, and in conflict with it. For instance: If, when instructing the ignorant, I prefer the doctrines of Mr. Wesley to those of Jesus and the apostles, then it is certain I am committing the sin of pride and self-preference.

"When they are comforting the afflicted, or provoking one another to love and good works, do they never perceive any inward self-commendation—*now you have done well?*" We answer: That as the word "commendation" means to speak in favor, and inward commendation to think in favor of, and as a man "should not think of himself more highly than he ought to think, but to think soberly," such as the author of these words did when he said, after thinking soberly: "As ye have us for ensamples," and "follow me as I follow Christ." May we not, therefore, inwardly feel, think and earnestly desire that others should follow us as we follow Christ; and this is inward commendation, thinking favorably of one's self in comparison with godless sinners, and if Satan suggests, *now you have done well*, when we have assisted one of his followers to turn against him and abandon his service, and accept of Christ's, we may respond yes, and thank God that he has condescended to use us instrumentally in the destruction of the kingdom of darkness. Thus we might continue to expose the sophistry and false reasoning upon Christian hearts and doctrines these two sermons contain, but we have said enough to show the extremity to which their author was driven to make out his theory.

Here Mr. Wesley declares that the sin in believers is chained so that it does not reign, and then goes on to specify its effects, as exemplified in thoughts, motives, feelings and actions, in every instance giving it living vitality.

If these are indeed guilty of having such sinful hearts, as those with which he endeavors to criminate them, they can have no claim of being Christ's followers or the children of God; "for if they were the children of God, they would do the works of God," and if they were ever converted, were now nothing but backsliders.

CHAPTER XI.

EXPERIENCE NO TEST OF DOCTRINE.

In this connection, we propose to reply to Mr. Wesley's objection against the doctrine that there is no sin in believers from the moment they are justified, " because it is contrary to the experience of the children of God." In answer to this objection we remark, that it is perfectly irrelevant to the case, because doctrines stand upon their own basis, and in the nature of the case cannot be affected by the experince of men.

If experience proves the truth of a doctrine, or system of doctrines, then the experience of the Jews proved the doctrines of Christ false, for as such they had no experience in harmony with them.

If such a supposition be admitted, then the experience of the Mohammedans proves their doctrines true, and those of Christianity false. So we might go through the whole list, but it seems only necessary thus to mention the absurdity, in order to demonstrate it to be such.

Jesus said, " I judge no man, but the words which I have spoken unto you, they shall judge you in the last day."

This, therefore, being the rule of judgment, by which sinners, who never had any Christian experience, as well as all others, are to be tried, justified or condemned, would have remained the same, and have been used for the same purpose, if no man ever had a Christian experience, and what is true of this, is also of every other doctrine of the Bible. And, therefore, if the Bible teaches the doctrine that God cleanses the heart of every one whom he receives, and at the time he receives him, then one of two things must follow, either that there is no uncleanness in the heart of a justified believer, unless he has backslidden, or that what man may fancy to be moral pollution, as in the instances we have examined of Mr. Wesley's views in regard to it, must be incorrect, and when rightly understood, will be found consonant with Christian purity as taught in the Bible.

For instance: After Jesus had said to his disciples, "Now ye are clean through the word which I have spoken unto you," no after experience of those disciples could prove that they were not clean at that time.

The experience of one of these who denied his Lord and master, and cursed and swore that he knew not the man, had no effect upon the fact that his heart was once clean every whit, nor the doctrine according to which it had been accomplished.

In order to show the absurdity of the supposition that experience is the test of the truth of a doctrine, we wish to introduce an instance in connection with this very doctrine.

We heard a man draw a comparison between the two blessings, one received at justification, and the other at sanctification, declaring the former to be but the few drops compared with the shower, and yet this man said he never knew when he was justified. It was when he was about ten years of age. The second blessing, according to him, was almost everything which was the result of his experience, judging from his stand-point.

The fact, however, in this case being, that he was never justified at all. When a child, he had been induced to join the church, sincere enough, no doubt, but had he drank the cup of repentance, realizing the nature of sin as others have done, and then been pardoned, would he not have remembered when it was? No wonder he should have found in his heart, because never converted at all, all the sin Mr. Wesley describes. But now he seeks sanctification, and receiving it as he supposes, but it is only justification in our apprehension. How differently he talks about conversion than Saul of Tarsus? How different his experience from millions of others, and the reason is obvious; he never had it when he supposed, and when he did receive it, as sanctification, as he understood it, no wonder it was the shower in comparison to the few drops, which in his childhood, he confounded with justification. Hence the delusion, that experience proves the truth of any doctrine.

In fact, the two ideas of doctrines and experience, are so dissimilar that they admit of no comparison; experience is that which a man feels or has felt, and relates to the heart or affections, while doctrines comprehend a system of ideas, and relate to the intellect.

All that experience can do in this direction is, to enable the man who has complied with the requirements of any doctrine, to know that he has thus complied. Hence it is said, *John* vii, 17: "If any man shall do his will, he shall know of the doctrine, whether it be of God, or whether I speak of myself." But we claim, what the advocates of sin in believers all concede, that the experience of all Christians is in harmony with our view, to the effect that no sin exists in the hearts of justified belivers, and never will be felt or experienced, unless they fall from grace; while Mr. Wesley admits that no sin is felt or experienced in any heart when justified; therefore all experience vindicates our position, and not Mr. Wesley's;—the only difference being, that he finds sin in the heart, not at the moment of justification, but at some period afterwards; while we agree with him in finding no sin in the heart at justification, but if we find it in the heart at some future period, it is the result of having left its first love; and while we call on such to return, repent, and do the first works over again, or receive the apostate's doom, Mr. Wesley's doctrine lulls them in the sleep of carnal security, by proclaiming to them that they are justified believers, and as such are sure of salvation; and that, in some mysterious way, God makes impure hearts pure, before taking them out of the world, even if they are killed by lightning; which is contrary to God's whole economy of grace—whose voice is to be ready at any and every moment for the transition of worlds. Is not the tendency of belief in such, fatally to encourage men to continue unholy in heart?

Just make them believe that they are justified, and, as such, sure of heaven; if taken out of the world, no matter by what casualty, or however suddenly, God will see to it and purify their hearts before sensibility is gone, or even afterwards, as long as life lasts.

Besides, if God can consistently thus cleanse the heart from impurity, what propriety or truth can there be in that feature of this theory, which makes it indispensable that this inward sin and impurity of heart shall be discovered, and he who possesses it required to mourn on the account of its existence, for quite a long period after conversion? Is God a respecter of persons, that he will do for a man struck by lightning what he will not for one who is not; that because one is going to die, he will cleanse him from the carnal mind, while another, who is not so soon to change worlds, he leaves this carnal mind, which is enmity against himself, in his heart for a longer period, and for what purpose God and man would be ashamed to tell?

The fact is, the whole theory casts a most sad reflection on the character of God, showing him to be inconsistent and partial, and consequently can have no other foundation than the mere fancy of a superstitious brain.

Another error from this fruitful source is, that if a Christian sins willfully after having been cleansed and made pure in heart, either partly or wholly, all his old depravity returns again into his soul. This is like all erroneous theories, one part destroys the other.

It is claimed that this unholy nature is inherited down from Adam through all generations. The very idea of inheritance being something transmitted from parents to children, or from other ancestors, demonstrates that the same thing cannot be inherited the second time by the same individual. Suppose a man inherits a farm from his ancestors, and that it is sunk by an earthquake, can he inherit it again? Or suppose he inherits consumption, and that by the application of skillful remedies he is partly or wholly cured; now, although he may take the consumption and die with it, yet he cannot inherit it, or that part of it which we have supposed cured.

Here is a man whose unholy nature, received from his ancestors and Adam, has been washed away by the blood of Jesus, but now he commits willful sin, is it not impossible that he should again inherit that same depravity which had been thus destroyed? He may become as depraved as ever, but is it not simply nonsense that it should be the second time inherited? But it is claimed that in some mysterious manner God sends all his old depravity again into the apostate's soul.

It must be borne in mind that that which God

sends again into such hearts is the carnal mind, and which "is enmity against God." Hence the monstrous idea that God infuses into the heart of every man, no matter how high has been his state of grace, whether partly or wholly purified from the carnal mind, that very carnal mind again, which in its very nature is enmity against himself. Does not the sinner who thus falls, and for whose recovery provision has been made thus—"If any man sin, we have an advocate with the Father, Jesus Christ the righteous"—hate God enough, without his especial interfering for the porpose of infusing into the fallen heart more of the principle of hatred against himself, a principle which "is not subject to the law of God, neither indeed can be?"

What would be thought even of a man who would act thus toward an enemy, who should take especial pains to make his enemy hate him with a more deadly hate than he would otherwise have done? But to implicate God with such conduct is nothing less than atrocious blasphemy, or else the result of consumate ignorance, for which there is neither Scripture, common sense or philosophy.

We now propose to examine Mr. Wesley's last argument in defence of his doctrine of sin in believers; and if we find it to fail as perfectly of its object, as all the others have done, we submit whether there is the least ground for its belief.

He says: "The opposite doctrine, that there is no sin in believers, is quite new in the church of Christ; for seventeen hundred years it was never heard of, till discovered by Count Zinzendorf; but whatever doctrine is new must be wrong; for the old is the only true one, and no doctrine can be right, unless it is the very same which was from the beginning."

We fully endorse the logic and truth of this proposition, and conclude, with Mr. Wesley, that if the doctrine we advocate is not older than the seventeenth century, and originated with Count Zinzendorf, or any other man, then it cannot be true. But we have fully proved that Jesus Christ and the apostles were the authors of the doctrine we adopt, and not Count Zinzendorf, and that it originated in the very infancy of the church of Christ, when composed of only twelve members, and not in the seventeenth century, as Mr. Wesley supposed; but was from the very beginning, and is therefore the true one.

It cannot be unreasonable that Mr. Wesley should be required to abide by his own logic, and therefore we turn the conclusion against himself, and say, whatever doctrine is new cannot be true; and we add, it must not be taught by garbling a few texts, but by the harmony of Scripture, as expounded, not by men, but by the sacred writers themselves, and leaving them to define the meaning of the words they use.

Having tried Mr. Wesley's doctrine of sin in believers by this standard, and found it wanting—utterly irreconcilable with Bible truth—and having searched the history of the church, from the days of Jesus till the present, without finding a single teacher or advocate of his doctrine, we can come to no other conclusion, than that it originated with himself, and therefore, not being from the beginning, and never heard of till the seventeenth century, it cannot be true.

CHAPTER XII.

OUR EXPERIENCE, AND THE EFFECTS OF THIS DOCTRINE

As it is supposed by some, although the notion is simply absurd, that this doctrine cannot be understood, only by those who have had the experience in harmony with it, we propose here to relate our own. In doing which, we shall be obliged to ask pardon for the use of the personal pronoun, I, which is more convenient:

I think it was in the year 1838, when the Rev. James Caughey was stationed at Lansingburgh, N. Y. There was a great revival of religion in the church where he preached. Many of my young friends were seeking and obtaining the favor of God. I became alarmed on the account of my sins, and for a number of days felt that if I let that opportunity pass without being converted, I would be lost. So deep was this conviction, that I was afraid to sleep nights, because of awful dreams of being among the lost at the judgment. Nevertheless, I strove to resist the conviction, and run the hazard of eternal ruin. With others I endeavored to get up a series of dances, for which I was passionately fond, for the winter, but through the providence of God, failed. I was dreadfully afraid to attend these meetings, but finally went. I may say here that I was about as wild and wicked a youth, of about twenty years, as I ever knew; such a profane swearer that I did not know when I did it; indeed, was prominent in almost every kind of wickedness.

After attending the meetings for a few nights, I resolved that when the invitation was given on the following one, I would go to the altar, and not as an experiment, but come what would, to be a Christian the remainder of my life.

I went three nights in succession, pleading with God to have mercy on me a sinner. So intent was I to be saved from sin, and the damnation of hell, that I hardly heard or noticed anything going on around me, till between nine and ten o'clock the third night, while in the most dreadful, mental and moral darkness I ever experienced, the heavens seeming like brass, I could not weep like others around me, and driven almost to despair, all at once, as in a moment, light, peace and joy unspeakable and full of glory broke in upon my soul; I was a new creature in Christ Jesus; for months I could sing

> "Jesus all the day long
> Was my joy and my song,
>   O! that all his salvation might see;
> He hath loved me, I cried,
> He hath suffered and died,
>   To redeem such a rebel as me."

At this time, our minister preached a course of sermons to the young converts, in the afternoons, on the subject of sanctification. Of course, he preached just as Mr. Wesley had taught, and portrayed the hearts of all merely justified believers as unclean, and pointed out the second blessing as the only remedy. He said we would all feel just as the poet sings, on making the discovery that our hearts were still unclean:

"O! that my load of sin were gone,
O! that I could at last submit;
Rest for my soul I long to find,
Saviour of all, if mine thou art." etc.

These sentiments, of course, were sung as applicable to justified believers instead of to penitent sinners, to whom they belong; those who had seen the spirituality of the law of God, and had not submitted to be governed by it, who had the yoke of inbred sin still crushing them with its guilty weight, and before receiving the yoke of Christ, which is easy, and which gives rest to the soul. "Take my yoke upon you, and learn of me, for I am meek and lowly in heart, and ye shall find rest to your souls, for my yoke is easy and my burden is light." Evidently, the yoke this poet sings about, and that Christ puts upon every converted sinner, are not the same. But supposing this hymn to be expressive of the justified heart, it went very far toward singing up the load, which was supposed to be sin.

We were recommended to read Carrevosa, Bramwell, Mrs. Fletcher, Esther Ann Rodgers, and to take the Guide to Christian Perfection·

with which I complied, and became thoroughly acquainted with Methodist literature on this subject. My peace and joy was now gone, and I had the fancied load of sin heavy enough upon my heart, and had fully determined to seek the second blessing. I sought it earnestly, but did not then obtain it.

About two years after this (I speak simply from memory as to the date), Bishop Hedding, who resided then in the village, preached in the afternoons on this subject, during the progress of another revival.

I was now well read on the subject, and fully understood and believed the doctrine, and became more engaged than ever for its attainment, seeking it day and night, and, like Mr. Bramwell, almost tortured myself in the effort; till at last, one evening at a prayer-meeting held at a private house, all at once I was was able to fill up, as the instruction was, with faith, the little distance between my suffering heart and the blessing I sought, and instantly received just what all the expounders described upon this subject; and the second blessing was mine, the load was gone, and my joy and peace returned, and I was as happy as when first converted, and no more so. Now came the duty of professing it specifically, on condition of retaining the evidence, if not the blessing itself; neither of which could I afford to lose; and therefore, the first opportunity that presented itself, I made the distinct profession by telling my experience. I now became an enthusiastic advocate of this doctrine. I seemed to see the church in a horrible condition, and became so intent on having it come up to this standard, that, to a great degree, I lost my interest in the salvation of sinners. If I began to pray for them, I soon found myself praying for the sanctification of the church. If I began to preach to sinners, I soon found myself preaching to a corrupt and unholy church.

The Rev. Benjamin Pomeroy at this time was stationed in Waterford, who, one evening, invited me to come over and preach for him, which I endeavored to do, from the text: "Is there no balm in Gilead; is there no physican there? Why, then, is the health of the daughter of my people not recovered?" The application I gave it was to a sickly and an unholy church, without the second blessing. The argument was this: You all acknowledge this blessing to be attainable, *and that now*, and that you would be more useful in the church, and able to set better examples before the world with than without it. Thus knowing your duty, can you retain your justified state, and refuse to make the offering of your whole heart to God? I contended they could not; that the omission of the duty involved guilt.

After I had finished, Brother Pomeroy exhorted, endorsing and enforcing the conclusion at which I had arrived, the result of which was, that all the Christians except myself and Brother B., and a few others, went from that meeting with the conviction, either that the doctrine preached was untrue, or that they were all guilty sinners.

This circumstance had the effect to strengthen me in my course on this subject. I did not attempt, as some do, to trim along between, and endeavor to please both parties, but drove the argument to its legitimate conclusion.

If the premises were correct, the conclusions

were inevitable. "He that knoweth to do good, and doeth it not, to him it is sin;" and all admitted that it was a good thing to get the heart cleansed from sin. Before I received this second experience, or my attention was called to it, there were frequent responses to my prayers and exhortations by the brethren generally, but now I noticed they only came from a few, and from those who before this I had not taken for the wisest and most consistent Christians, but they had the peculiar views with myself, and we formed a class in the church; and many of these had to be converted over again about every year, or every six months. In fact, I found, so far as my observation went, that it was the most ignorant and unreliable who made this profession.

My charity for all my brethren was now considerably circumscribed, including very few others than those who either had or were seeking this blessing. I moved along, crying "O! that my head were waters, and mine eyes a fountain of tears, that I might weep day and night for the slain of the daughter of my people," giving the passage this application and construction. I had the charity which endured all things, except a word against the doctrine of the second blessing.

I thought the apostle was either speaking for effect, or for some purpose which I could not comprehend, when he said: "Let every one esteem others better than themselves," as I did not suppose any one could be better than myself, and indeed none were so good who did not possess the second blessing. As for babes in Christ, there were none, for all but these peculiar few were living in the open omission of a known and acknowledged duty, and were thus gulity in the sight of God; and my class were the only one who could pray effectually for them. The church was utterly unprepared to feed and nourish young converts, and it were about as well they were not converted and brought into it, if they were to take the example of the great majority, and live with hearts full of sin.

As for other denominations, my only hope was that they would all become Methodists, and that the Methodists would all come up to this standard of what I then supposed to be sanctification. If there seemed to be any conflict between the views of Mr. Wesley and the doctrines of Jesus upon this subject, the man's were always preferred. If a revival was commenced, I always began to pray and exhort the church to get sanctified, without which there could be but little hope of the conversion of sinners; of course, this was never realized, and therefore I was always gloomy and disappointed on such occasions. If I dreaded any one sentiment more than another, it was that of attaining the second blessing by degrees, through a period of years.

With such views and feelings, I found everything to be confusion; before this I was happy, and had charity for all Christians, but now all was contest and disappointment; I became almost discouraged because so few would come up to my standard, and especially so few of the intelligent and the straightforward of the church. This was marvelous. Under these circumstances I began to reflect, and resolved to review the whole subject, and to ascertain, if possible, the real grounds for the doctrine. I laid aside all the Methodist literature and human opinion, going directly to the Bible, and to that alone, to see if indeed its doctrines, I had thus adopted, corresponded with it, the result of which we have given in this little work.

But now the question arose: How can you account for your experience of the second blessing? The answer was simple and easy, and may be explained in a few words.

When I was first converted, I felt and knew that there was a complete change of heart. I had not the faintest idea that anything remained to be done to make it any more pure. Such was my experience and conviction until I heard this doctrine preached, which described my heart, as well as those of all others in a mere justified state, as being still depraved with inherent sin, left there at conversion, called "moral pollution," "remains of the carnal mind," "roots of bitterness," etc.

Such were the ambiguous terms used to describe it, that no definite idea was conveyed. Had the preacher, or an angel from heaven, declared that there was, what the carnal mind signifies, "enmity against God" in my heart,

I would have instantly repelled the idea as false. But thus portraying the heart, and having the utmost confidence in the preacher's goodness and ability, the result was, as he described I felt, receiving every word as truth. He said I would find a load of sin, which was original sin, and which would depress my soul; and it came just as he said. It was also said, I would get relieved of it in the manner already indicated, and so I did. Now I say, that this feeling was produced by mental hallucination. The load of sin, so called, was preached into my heart, and, according to the other feature of the psychological impression, preached out again, when relieved from it, and which I supposed was the second blessing, and in either case the spirit or truth of God had nothing whatever to do; for "the spirit and the word agree." And as we have seen, that the word of God is perfectly irreconcilable with this theory, therefore it was only to be accounted for upon this well-known law of mind: that of impression according to what the mind believes to be the truth, whether it is or not. When I was thus relieved, I was just where I was before hearing this error preached. This philosophy is thus explained by Paul: "As a man thinketh, so is he." This load of depression, received upon this principle, may be illustrated thus: Suppose a man away from home and his property, and hears, from a source of unquestionable veracity, that his property and family are all engulfed in an earthquake, or destroyed in any other way; would he not immediately be overwhelmed with intense depression of spirit? But on returning home, he finds the report to have been false, finding everything as he left; would not his depressive load instantly be gone, and his heart leap for joy at the discovery?

So it was with me. Before hearing this second conversion doctrine preached, I felt I had a great possession, which made me happy from day to day; but when I heard this bad and erroneous doctrine preached, my happiness was gone. But when I found it a deception, not founded upon the teachings of Jesus, the apostles and prophets, the psychological hallucination vanished, and of course my peace and joy returned again. This was the result of my investigation. The error produced the same effect, as long as it was believed to be truth, as though it were such.

The conclusion at which we arrive, in order to account for the experience for others in the church, in relation to this doctrine, may be summed up thus:

First, there is one class joins the church, either from deception or design, or both, who are never converted at all. Some of them supposing themselves to have been converted, and yet dissatisfied with their experience, are induced to seek what is taught as being sanctification. Now being in earnest, God receives them, but it is only the first, not the second blessing. This is their conversion, and it is so vast a change in comparison with what they ever had before, that they speak of it accordingly.

Another class who seek this blessing, are those who have become backslidden in heart from God, and all do this who leave their first love, and who must return and repent, or perish, and being reclaimed profess it as the second blessing, their backslidings are healed, and God again loves them freely. But instead of its being a higher state of purity than that which they enjoyed when first converted, they are simply restored to that.

Then there is another class who have never taken their hearts out of Christ's keeping, they have always taken heed to the injunction "abide in me," and his words have remained in them, and they have been kept in the same sanctified state, as when Jesus said unto them, "Now ye are clean through the words I have spoken unto you."

These may be deluded by the false doctrine of the impurity of all mere justified believers, supposing themselves unclean in heart, when they are not, and induced to seek deliverance from it, under the hallucination of the error, and experience what they suppose is the second blessing, but which leaves them no purer than when first converted.

This class will never be heard belittling their conversion, and the reason why, is simply because they had one, which to them and all others, is a perfect moral resurrection from the dead. To such, " Old things are passed away, and behold, all things are become new." These three classes, scripturally and philosophically, fully accounts for all the experience there is in relation to this doctrine. If there was nothing more to prove it an error, than the fact that it makes schism and divisions of heart in the church, this alone would be conclusive; indeed it has reached such a height that it is almost impossible to work in harmony with those who labor under this delusion. Their history in the past has been when this disaffection has culminated; they have broken off from the unholy membership in small parties, and set up for themselves, there has, however, never been religion enough among them to live together in Christian fellowship but for very short periods. It would seem that if they were as holy as they suppose and profess to be, such would not have been the case. And does not this historic fact demonstrate that they are not in spirit and faith, those who compose the church "founded upon the apostles and prophets, Jesus Christ himself being the chief corner stone," and against which he declared "the gates of hell shall not prevail?" The gates of hell have always prevailed against their efforts to form churches, and in a little while they are found individually creeping back again among the unholy. But their plan now seems changed, and they are going to take the church by storm, and it is a storm; and suppose they should, would there be any more union and brotherly love among them, than when alone in separate organizations?

But we believe that this very effort will prove the utter extermination of the evil. It will be another example of Satan over-doing himself. Its features have became so intolerant that it compels the reconsideration of the whole question, which is hereafter to be, not when are justified believers to experience this second blessing, but is the doctrine true, and Jesus and the apostles, and not Mr. Wesley or any other authors, are to decide as to what is truth? The question must be met upon its merits. The parties are distinct, and more so in heart than in theory, we mean in theory up to the present time,

The attempt to trim along between these, and to try to make it appear both are right, is simply absurd, the only tendency of which is to feed the fires, and such displease both sides vastly more than though they fearlessly defined their position.

Another of the tactics of these deluded people is to gather at all the camp-meetings a few from each church, coming from great distances, make a multitude, and when there, nothing can be heard but this erroneous theory; here it appears in its most offensive form.

The ministers of our day who embrace this peculiar view, are generally of the lower grade of intellect, and especially the poorer students of the Bible; you hear them appeal oftener to our standard authors than to Jesus and Paul. They generally take possession of our revivals, and as a class they are far from being our firm, straightforward, intelligent Christian membership, whose example is salutary in community; and if sustained by the preacher in charge, by sympathizing with their views, the real intelligent Christians of the church are put upon the anxious seat. Come to the altar with your corrupt, filthy and bad hearts, and we will pray for you, are the addresses they make. Thus are they kept back from taking part in these meetings. This is not the case in any other church but ours. The revivals there are carried on by the business men in the community, the men of consistency and power.

But we submit this little work, feeling confident that it will have some influence in restraining the march of this worst error in the whole Protestant church at the present day, and indeed the only troublesome thing in ours. We have no sympathy with luke-warm or cold-hearted Christianity. The whole church should be warned to return to their first love, where all was interest; all was aglow with love; all was labor for the salvation of others. Give no quarters to the sentiment, that those who have fallen from this state of single-eyed purity are, nevertheless, justified believers. Under the preaching of this truth, we may expect to see such a revival as we have never before witnessed.

We fearlessly put the truth of God against the errors of men, between which, if there is conflict, we unhesitatingly adopt the declaration: "Let God be true, but every man a liar."

www.ingramcontent.com/pod-product-compliance
Lightning Source LLC
Chambersburg PA
CBHW021354230426
43666CB00006B/521